Shocking Celebrity Murders Vol. 3

True Crime Cases of Famous People Who Were Gruesomely Killed

Jack Smith

Warning
Throughout the book, there are some descriptions of murders and crime scenes that some people might find disturbing. There might be also some language used by people involved in the murders that may not be appropriate.

Note
Words in italic are quoted words from verbatim and have been reproduced as is, including any grammatical errors and misspelled words.

ISBN 9798390951705

Printed in the United States

Contents

They're Rich, They're Famous, and They're Dead

Hollywood has held an allure since the early 20th Century as an almost mythical place in which just about anything is possible. Fortune, fame, and for the unfortunate few—death by homicide. Yes, Hollywood has long been the source of both dreams and nightmares. This book takes a look at some accounts of those who have found themselves delving into the darker side of Hollywood.

Just take the case of Carl Switzer. He was once the most adorable child star in Hollywood when he reprised the role of "Alfalfa" in "The Little Rascals." As an adult however, Carl could barely find work and resorted to odd jobs and even criminal activity—such as illegally chopping down a bunch of pine trees so he could sell them to eager seekers of authentic Christmas trees.

It was sheer and utter desperation that drove Carl Switzer to engage in activities that put him at risk, and he reaped the consequences. He was shot at a bar and was later murdered by an enraged associate during a drunken altercation.

As much promise as the young Carl showed in Hollywood, he slid into its dark underbelly in his later years and was never able to resurface. Sal Mineo faced a strikingly similar fate. He came to fame starring alongside the likes of James Dean in "Rebel without a Cause" but by the 1970s he was washed up and out of work. He was later found dead in his parking lot—apparently gunned down by a local drug dealer.

The life of actress Christina Helm didn't end much better. Christina, with her beauty and charm, was on the verge of becoming the next great thing when she was viciously assaulted in the middle of the street. Moments later, she was found crumpled up in a pool of blood, breathing her last breath.

In the meantime, John Lennon, founder of the Beatles, ended up slain by one of his own deranged fans. The fan stalked him and watched his every movement, before simply walking up to the former Beatle and opening fire. The attacker had no reason at all to kill the superstar other than the fact that he was there—*and he was famous.*

Certainly, a terrible way for anyone's life to end, and even more shocking to have such things happen to the rather elite Hollywood celebrities. All of the famous celebrities presented in this book, all met a sudden and grisly end. Yes, they were rich, and yes, they were famous, but all of them met a dreadful fate. This book touches upon the details of their lives and the circumstances that led to their untimely demise.

Lord Byron's Death During the Greek Revolution

Who*:* Lord Byron
Where: Greece
When: April 1824
Suspects*:* Unknown
Conviction*:* None

Background Information

Lord Byron was a legendary and romantic figure. The fact that he gave his life for the cause of the Greek Revolution in 1824, only served to bolster that image even further in the minds of many. Byron was born on 22 January 1788. He was the son of Captain John Byron and Catherine Gordon, a wealthy heiress.

His parents' relationship was tumultuous. His dad was a sailor often away at sea, and his mother was a wealthy heiress. His father obtained some fame for his able maneuvering of watercraft on the high seas but unfortunately was always somehow running short of funds. Therefor Byron's frustrated mother often ended up footing his father's many bills. In fact, she financed his last trip when the elder Byron sailed off to France in 1798.

Shortly thereafter Captain John Byron passed away from a bad and lingering case of tuberculosis. This left Catharine to raise her then 10-year-old child all by herself. Since her son was suddenly the only thing she had left, Catherine understandably fixated on him. It's said that she alternately spoiled and nitpicked at her son—never really just letting him be.

And as much as she showered him with gifts, she could also be bitingly cruel. Such as the time she called him a "lame brat" apparently taunting the fact that he had been born with an abnormality in his foot. But nevertheless, she was in her son's corner when it mattered. And it was her love, support (and money) that sent the younger Byron off to the best schools that Britain could provide. He attended the prestigious Harrow School where he distinguished himself as a good student as well as a great athlete.

He used his accolades at this school as a springboard to attend Trinity College in Cambridge. He was a great student and received much acclaim for his poetry. After his studies, Byron pursued writing professionally, and by 1812 he had become famous and well-known. In his day, he was indeed a celebrity. Shortly thereafter he traveled the world, seeing places far and wide.

Included in his travels was Greece which at that time was still a province of the Ottoman Empire. The mighty Ottomans was an Islamic empire that rose up in Asia Minor (Modern Day Turkey) in the 14th Century. At the time of the Ottomans' rise, the Greek-speaking Byzantine Empire, which was based outside Constantinople (modern-day Istanbul) in Asia Minor, was still the greatest power in the region.

But that soon changed as the Ottoman Turks continued to steadily chip away at Byzantine possessions. In 1453 the Ottomans stormed the capital of the once-great Greek Empire of the Byzantines. Constantinople was conquered, and this former Christian Orthodox capital of the Greek-speaking world was transformed into Istanbul. Asia Minor, which used to be the province of the Greeks, was turned into modern-day "Turkey."

The Turks were not finished, however, and as they pushed onward into the Balkans, they eventually made their way to Greece itself. At the time of Byron's journey, Greece was still reeling under Ottoman Oppression. With the encouragement of many a European intellectual, who was madly in love with ancient Greek culture, the Greeks were encouraged to finally shake off the Ottoman yoke.

In the past, this was not possible—even wholesale Crusades launched by the church could not shake loose the Ottomans' grip. But by the early 1800s, the situation had changed, and the Ottoman Empire nicknamed the "Sick man of Europe" was well past its prime. As such, the Greeks were encouraged to rise up and regain their freedom. In the 1820s they finally got serious about it and Lord Byron was one of the leading intellectual celebrities leading the charge.

In 1823, he put his words where his mouth was, heading over to Greece in person. He sailed from the port of Genoa on a ship called—fittingly enough—*The Hercules.* He arrived in Greece that July and was soon instructed as to what was expected of him. The trouble, however, was that the leadership of the Greek rebels was so hopelessly fractured that Byron soon had multiple people giving him multiple different directives.

There were essentially several voices shouting at him all at once, as each leader of each rebel group tried to make Lord Byron their spokesperson. Byron ultimately ended up throwing in his hat with one "Alexandros Mavrokordatos" who were a budding Greek statesman and eager political militant. Through his contacts with Alexandros, Byron raised arms and money for the cause. In fact, he ended up selling his own English estate to help fund the war.

Along with putting his money where his mouth was, Byron was also eager to put his own boots onto the ground. In furtherance of these efforts, he was put in charge of his own military unit—the so-called "Byron Brigade." Ironically enough, it would not be on the battlefield that the great poet and hopeless romantic Lord Byron would die.

On That Day

Before he could ever engage in active combat on the battlefield, Lord Byron would succumb to an altogether invisible enemy. Due to poor environmental conditions where he was stationed, Byron got horribly sick from a terrible illness he had contracted. He suffered a raging hot fever from this mysterious disease and ultimately died on 19 April 1824.

Although the official cause of his death is listed as being due to this outbreak of illness, there are some who have openly wondered if perhaps he had somehow met with foul play. Not everyone liked Byron's efforts in Greece after all, and there were some who just might have wanted him out of the picture. The Turks obviously didn't like this outsider stirring up the Greeks. Even more important, there were *some Greeks* who didn't want him there either!

The Suspects

The source of this disenchantment with Byron was the rivalries among the Greek leaders. According to Lord Byron's own physician, Julius van Millingne, there was some talk among various rebel factions of making Lord Bryon "King of Greece" should he successfully lead the rebellion against the Ottomans. This was a threat to just about every other rebel faction, since the group who made Byron King, no doubt would have had considerable political clout.

Ever since the days of the Byzantine Empire, Greek politics had been rife with incessant plots and intrigue. Therefore "Byzantine" is often used as an expression to describe a complicated bit of intrigue and subterfuge. Just think of someone stating: "He just couldn't figure out the cause of such bizarre, Byzantine machinations!"

In The End

At any rate, there was indeed much plotting and intriguing among the Greek rebel factions, and not all of them were on board with the idea of Lord Byron being King. And they most certainly did not want him to be crowned by their political rivals. So, yes, not all of the Greeks involved might have liked this idea—but would the very possibility push someone to target and kill Lord Byron? As it stands, we might never really know for sure.

Edgar Allan Poe
A 19th-Century Celebrity
Gone Wrong

Who*:* Edgar Allan Poe
Where: Baltimore, Maryland
When: October 1849
Suspects*:* Reynolds - Unknown
Conviction*:* None

Background Information

Edgar Allen Poe's writings are well known. Most either love them or hate them - with very few falling in between. Mr. Poe was born in Boston, Massachusetts, on 19 January 1809. He was the son of actor David Poe and his actress wife, Elizabeth "Eliza" Poe.

At the time of Edgar's birth, his father David still had plenty of ambition for himself, but that ambition simply did not include child-rearing. As such, he soon left the family, forcing his wife and son to fend for themselves. Even worse for the young Edgar was that the following year his mother, Elizabeth, suddenly passed away.

Considering the unknown whereabouts of his absent dad, this essentially made Edgar an orphan. Was it not for the kindness of John and Frances Allan, who resided in Richmond Virginia, he would have been almost entirely on his own. Although this couple never made their adoption of Edgar official, they raised Edgar until he reached young adulthood.

With the encouragement of his adoptive parents, he attended the University of Virginia, but he ended up dropping out when he couldn't afford to pay for tuition. However, the real problem was that the young Edgar picked up the habit of gambling. For as soon as his adoptive father John Allan sent him money, Edgar gambled it away. Edgar Allan Poe, seemingly lost, listless, and without direction, then did what confused young men have done for centuries - he joined the army.

He signed up with the U.S. military in 1827. While he was still in the armed forces, he wrote his first known anthology of poetry, which he dubbed, "Tamerlane and Other Poems." In the meantime, Edgar and John Allan seemed to reconcile with each other in 1829, after the abrupt passing of John's wife, Frances. Frances was the closest thing to a mother that Edgar Allan Poe ever had, and both likely mourned the loss deeply.

Poe sought to further his military career, then went on to West Point. But despite his best efforts, his heart just wasn't in it, and he soon dropped out. He was able to use his ability as a writer to find work, however, getting hired for a literary journal, in which he served as a "literary critic." He made a living by writing critical reviews of the work of others - but what he really wanted to do was to write his own work. It wasn't a dream job, but it paid the bills. The work he did, however, had him on the move, as he bounced from one city to another to render his critical critiques.

In 1836 Poe perhaps shocked some of his surviving relatives when he decided to marry his 13-year-old cousin, Virginia Clemm. Such things were not entirely unheard of, but even then, the fact that she was so young - let alone his cousin - did indeed raise some eyebrows. In 1845 Poe wrote his epic poem, *The Raven*.

This poem reflects love, life, and terrible loss. Such things were no doubt on his mind at the time, since his wife had since become gravely ill. She had a bad case of tuberculosis, which she would ultimately die from in 1847. Two years later Poe himself ended up deceased under entirely bizarre circumstances.

On That Day

His last days are indeed still shrouded in much mystery. But here's a general synopsis of what is known. On 3 October 1849, Edgar Allan Poe was found basically laying in the streets of Baltimore, moaning unintelligibly and crying out loud.

It was hard not to miss this sad, strange sight, and passersby took notice. But then, as is often enough the case, most simply didn't want to get involved. Passersby just kept walking by. Eventually, his good Samaritan arrived and he was finally picked up off the ground by a doctor - Joseph W Walker - and carried off to "Washington Medical College."

It was here where he would ultimately last breathed out - perishing just a few days later on 7 October 1849. Among some of the odder details of his death was the fact that he was wearing strange clothing that did not seem to belong to him and that he was oddly rambling strange names and phrases. Among the words that he repeated was the name of "Reynolds."

For an even more dramatic flourish, the doctor who attended to him to his last claimed that his final utterance was a cry of "Lord help my poor soul!" In the midst of all of his rambling, this last definitive statement to his maker was perhaps the only clear thing that Poe said leading up to his death.

The Suspects

Interestingly enough, due to the fact that Poe was drunk and dressed in an odd outfit completely uncharacteristic of anything that he would have ever worn - a theory has developed as to what might have happened to him. For - so some have claimed - his state had all the hallmarks of someone who had been sucked into committing electoral malfeasance.

Interestingly enough, the day that he was found sprawled out on the ground in a drunken ramble, was indeed an election day. So what gives? Why would some then jump to the conclusion that Poe had been hoodwinked into casting bad ballots? Well, it seems that back in those days it was common for political operatives to coerce and sometimes even force random people to pay their respects to the ballot box multiple times.

These repeat, electoral offenders, achieved this feat by wearing a different outfit each and every single time they cast a ballot. It seems absurd and ridiculous, but apparently, this really did go on back in the 1800s. And the fact that Poe was found in an entirely odd and uncharacteristic getup which included a straw hat, such as a farmer (not a horror writer) would wear, seemed to suggest that he was indeed decked out in some sort of disguise.

Those who applied pressure to their marks to vote for their candidates supposedly plied them with drinks. Sometimes they even forced alcohol down their throats. All of this, so that they could be easily manipulated into providing their "electoral input" on multiple occasions through the course of an election day.

Such a bizarre set of circumstances can really get one's mind daydreaming about the strange situation that Poe might have found himself in. One could imagine horror writer Edgar Allan Poe (perhaps literally) strongarmed by some political operative, who shoves a ballot in his hand and a bottle in his mouth.

In The End

Before he passed, Poe repeated the name of "Reynolds." Could this Reynolds have had something to do with such a horrid encounter? Whatever the case may be, upon leaving this world, hopefully, the tortured soul of Edgar Allan Poe finally found some sense of peace.

Was It the Real McCoy?
The Sad Story of Kid McCoy

Who: Kid McCoy (Norman Selby)
Where: New York
When: December 1940
Suspects: Himself - Unknown
Conviction: None

Background Information

Born "Norman Selby" on 13 October 1872 in the sleepy Indiana town of Moscow, Indiana, Kid McCoy literally had a "train-hopping" youth. Moscow, a town in southeastern Indiana, is incredibly small and remote, even today boasting a population of only around 100 people. And it was even smaller and more remote when Norman Selby AKA the "Kid McCoy" was growing up.

It remains a little unclear exactly how he later developed the name "Kid McCoy", but the "kid" part was likely in reference to his youthful looks. For long after he was grown, he continued to maintain a rather childlike (some might even say downright cherubic), boyish appearance. This is despite the fact that Kid McCoy never really had much of a childhood, to begin with.

About as soon as he could walk, he was heading over to the train tracks to hitch a ride on trains headed out east to Cincinnati, Ohio. Yes indeed, in a small Indiana town like Moscow, the only attraction was likely the train tracks that brought trains from far and wide, through this little slice of the middle of nowhere.

These trains no doubt held out much promise to Selby of the wider world and what might await him outside of Moscow, Indiana. It was this glimmer of hope he saw on those tracks that had him hopping on trains, to hitch a ride to parts unknown. It was while he was doing all of this exploring, however, that he managed to get into quite a few fights in between.

As a rule, since one never knows who else might be stowing away on a train, a train hopper has to be on his guard. And Norman Selby apparently learned from a young age how to become a rough and ready fighter.

By his late teens, he sought to channel his fighting prowess, and at 18 years of age, he embarked on a career as a boxer.

Remaining entirely undefeated for his first few years in the ring, he was a force to be reckoned with. He delivered a devastating knockout punch and had a signature swing that utilized a twisting "corkscrew" type motion, that would almost always catch his opponents by surprise. And yes, one can only imagine that

McCoy likely learned this devastating punch all those times he had to fend off overgrown train hobos when he was a kid! You better believe anyway - no hobo would steal a can of pork and beans under his watch!

The kid was growing up fast and by the early 1890s, he was well known. So well known in fact, it's said that the expression, "the real McCoy" was derived from an allusion to Kid's excellent boxing skills. It's said that at some point, Kid McCoy was in a bar and got into an altercation with another patron. The guy proceeded to give the Kid a hard time, prompting someone else nearby to warn the apparently ignorant drunk that he was about to go toe to toe with the formidable boxing champ Kid McCoy.

The drunk didn't believe him, however, and laughed, "Yeah! And I'm George Washington!" Kid McCoy then promptly punched the guy out, and when the man recovered, he was heard to have muttered in astonishment, "By golly! *It was* the *real McCoy*!" It remains unclear if the incident really happened exactly as described, but the expression is indeed derived from this story (real or imagined) all the same.

McCoy was a guy known to play coy both in and outside the ring. Unlike a lot of other braggarts who want to boost themselves and make themselves seem tougher than they really are, Kid McCoy had the opposite strategy. He tried hard to make folks underestimate him. Just before a fight, he would often act weak and even physically ill in order to trick his opponent into thinking that he was a pushover—but Kid McCoy was only pretending.

For as soon as his opponent tried to lay a hand on him, he was waylaid with punch after devastating punch, until finally, that quick, signature corkscrew hook sent them down for the count. McCoy was the kind of guy who, if a big bully was hassling him, would act like he was afraid - *Oh please don't hurt me, big guy! Please don't hurt me!* Only for him to suddenly turn around and knock his overconfident (and entirely unsuspecting) opponent clean out.

It was a working strategy that served him well. He would act like a meek and mild weakling, only to suddenly give his adversaries the surprise of their life when he blasted them into oblivion with his fists. But some of McCoy's antics were a bit much - and some would say he took his schtick just a bit too far. As was the case in 1896 when he actually pretended that he was dying of cancer, before taking on champ Tommy Ryan.

Ryan was hoodwinked by McCoy's ploy and actually felt sorry for him. So much so, that he was even considering throwing the match and letting McCoy win on purpose, just so Kid McCoy could pay his doctor's bills. But the thing is - *there were no doctor's bills.* Because McCoy was lying. He wasn't sick at all. It was stuff like this that would have both critics and fans alike questioning the morality of Kid McCoy.

For it was one thing to play a little coy before a match, but a whole different story to pretend you have a terminal illness! Nevertheless, McCoy fought on. And he ended up finishing his run in the boxing ring on top. In 1914 he won his last round when he defeated Mathew Curran in London, England. This victory allowed him to retire at the top of his game.

But outside the ring, McCoy was not all that successful. He had a string of failed marriages and unsuccessful attempts at making a name for himself in business. He ended up getting married and divorced eight times, and delving into countless businesses and get-rich-quick schemes.

None of it seemed to work, however, and by the early 1920s, it's said that a down-on-his-luck McCoy was a drunk and a dead beat unable to make money. He soon had even more problems when he began an affair with a woman by the name of Teresa Mors.

Ms. Mors was married to a wealthy antique dealer and yet was attracted by the charms of the real McCoy himself. But shortly into their fling, Teresa turned up dead with a gunshot wound to her head. Soon thereafter he arrived at his sister Jennie Thomas' residence intoxicated and entirely out of sorts with himself. She would later claim that she heard him remark that he "just had to kill that woman."

If Jennie thought that her brother might sober up by morning, she would have to think again. McCoy had apparently really lost his mind. Instead of sobering up and becoming rational (and perhaps remorseful), he awakened with a vengeance. He was seen bright and early with a gun in hand, barging out of his sister's home and heading straight to the antique store of the woman he had just slain.

Apparently, no one knew the fate of Ms. Mors yet, and the shop employees were just getting ready to open up. Kid McCoy barged right in and started causing trouble. Bizarrely enough, he had a music box with him (perhaps swiped from his sister's pad?), and to the utter shock and amazement of those in front of him, opened it and danced to the music it played.

When the music ended, Kid turned his gun on the employees and began making demands. He demanded cash, but one of the workers made some sort of "sudden motion" that the Kid did not like, so he opened fire, hitting the guy in the leg. Kid McCoy then fled on foot. In the street, he was flagged down by a certain Mr. And Mrs. Sam Schapp who had seen him around the neighborhood before. Mr. Schapp, full of concern for the Kid, asked him, "Norman, what the hell are you doing?"

To this inquiry, Norman the Kid McCoy Selby unequivocally responded with a hail of bullets. Both Sam and his wife were hit. But Kid McCoy's rampage was not yet quite over. For next he went to a nearby park where he proceeded to take pot shots at random people who simply had the misfortune of passing by.

Incredibly enough, none of those injured in this rampage died - otherwise Norman Selby could very well have been classified as a serial killer. Despite the fact that they were rattled and shaken and some of them had bullets in their arms, legs, wrists, and feet, they survived. Norman Selby in the meantime, was arrested. And although he was clearly unhinged, he adamantly denied shooting Ms. Mors, claiming that she had shot herself.

Nevertheless, he was never charged with murder and was only convicted of manslaughter. For this, he would serve just a few years at San Quentin where he was noted as a model prisoner. He was released in 1932 and began working as an athletic director for the automaking giant Ford. He also became a kind of motivational speaker, talking at various venues about the "evils of strong drink".

On That Day

It was in the midst of one of these very tours in April 1940 that Norman the "Kid McCoy" Selby was found dead in a hotel room. He had a suicide note on hand, which ended with the sad refrain, "To all my dear friends - best of luck. Sorry I could not endure this world's madness." Most took Norman at his word and assumed he just got tired of life and was looking to make his exit. But there are those that have openly wondered if he was perhaps murdered.

In the End

Did someone have it out for the real McCoy? An ex-associate? An ex-inmate? Was he killed to avenge what happened to Teresa Mors? There are still a lot of questions about whatever happened to the Real McCoy.

Kurt Cobain's Suicide
Or Was it Murder?

Who: Kurt Cobain
Where: Seattle, Washington
When: April 1994
Suspects: Himself - Courtney Love
Conviction: None

Background Information

After Nirvana front man Kurt Cobain was found dead in his Seattle home in 1994, most accepted the official version of events - after a long battle with both depression and drug addiction, this moody and unstable musician chose to take his own life. This account is so widely accepted that in fact, for a while suicide and Kurt Cobain seemed darn near synonymous.

It reached a point where one could hardly even hear the name Kurt Cobain without thinking of suicide. And there is of course plenty of reason for that. Given the fact that one of Kurt's last recorded songs was titled "I Hate Myself and Want to Die", many were not even all that surprised. But was Kurt really a case of art imitating life? Did the guy who wrote so many depressing songs - many of them even referencing suicide -really end up taking his own life?

Or was that just an extremely convenient story to cover up something else? To conceal murder? Interestingly enough, that's precisely what one of Kurt's closest family members thought. Kurt was actually very close to his paternal grandparents, Leland and Ira Cobain. One might not think as much, due to the Nirvana song Sliver, which has Kurt thinking back to a troubled childhood in which he was being babysat by his grandparents.

In the song, after running through lyrics that perfectly (amazingly really) capture the trauma of being separated from one's parents and left with relatives one hardly knows, we hear Kurt's plaintive chorus as he pleads, "Grandma, take me home! Grandma, take me home!"

Nevertheless, Kurt biographer Ian Halparin conducted extensive interviews with Kurt's grandfather, Leland, in the early 2000s, and was stunned to find that Kurt's beloved grandfather was absolutely convinced that his grandson, Kurt Cobain, had been straight-up murdered. But by who? The most commonly cited suspect is the woman who was Kurt's wife at the time - Courtney Love.

Mrs. Love was the subject of Ian's book "Love & Death" which suggested that perhaps Courtney Love had more to do with Kurt's demise than most have previously thought. Not only that,

Ian conducted interviews with Courtney's dad, Hank Harrison, a man who also openly considered the possibility. It is indeed pretty damning for one to have your own father think you could be a killer. So, what gives?

In order to understand how a parent could reach such a conclusion about his own child, we need a little bit of background on Courtney herself. Courtney Love came from a turbulent home. Her parents are often described as classic hippies who had her at a young age, and from the start, failed to give her enough attention.

When she was born, Courtney's parents were young, free spirits, and didn't like being bothered by the responsibilities of parenting. And often they didn't bother. After Courtney's parents split up, her mother often foisted Courtney on whatever friends would take her. It was when Courtney's mom ran out of options, that she ended up with her dad. Courtney and her father's relationship was originally quite good, but by the time Courtney was in her teens, they had drifted apart.

Courtney and her father both seem to have equal parts animosity for each other and have both said terrible things about one another. But there's no denying that Courtney was a troubled kid. She ran the streets and was often in and out of trouble. So clearly Courtney Love had her problems, but was she troubled enough to bump off Kurt?

First, let's consider the circumstances of the Nirvana front man's final few moments on Earth. According to the official account of Kurt's last days, he was on tour in Europe in March 1994, when he began suffering from problems with his throat. Kurt was known to have health problems for much of his life - whether they originated in his stomach, lungs, or as some might suggest his mind. So this wasn't at all unusual.

At any rate, it was in the midst of this bronchial flare-up that Kurt flew off to Rome, where he met up with Courtney. On 3 March Love claims to have woken up to find her husband unresponsive. It seems that he had ingested a large number of sleeping pills. Was this his first suicide attempt? As some have claimed? Kurt recovered and returned stateside shortly thereafter.

Interestingly enough, however, for those back in the United States, it was not immediately clear what happened to Kurt or if he was even still alive. Rock journalist Danny Goldberg, who actively followed the Cobains, would later recall that he actually received a phone call from record company guru David Geffen shortly after the incident, in which Geffen was certain that Cobain was dead.

Goldberg recalls Geffen starting up the conversation by sadly stating, "Well, there are some people who just can't be helped no matter what you do." He was apparently talking about Kurt as if he was already grieving his loss. Goldberg, who had just talked to Courtney and had been fully briefed on the matter, pushed back a bit, insisting Kurt would be fine. Geffen then cut him off by abruptly stating, "Danny, he's dead. Courtney just called me and told me he's dead."

These cutting remarks obviously must have created a lot of confusion between the two men. But as Goldberg reveals, the matter was cleared up when it was realized that whoever Geffen had talked to—*wasn't Courtney.* Geffen and Goldberg later surmised that he was the victim of a prank caller.

But oddly enough, Geffen was indeed initially quite certain he had spoken to Courtney. So who was it? Did Geffen get pranked by a morbid and strangely perceptive fan who was somehow aware of Kurt's rough shape, or was Courtney herself playing a strange game with them all?

If we go down that rabbit whole, we can come to some rather chilling conclusions. Could it be that Courtney thought Kurt was dead at some point, and preemptively phoned Geffen? Then when she realized he would pull through, did she have to reverse course and call up Danny Goldberg? This is still not exactly clear.

At any rate, it wasn't long after Kurt's return to the United States that trouble began anew. On 8 March Courtney Love called up the Seattle police department to let them know that Kurt had been talking of suicide and had apparently locked himself up in a room with a loaded gun. Upon their arrival, however, Kurt told the cops that Love was lying, that he wasn't at all suicidal and he was simply taking protective measures to get away from his wife, Courtney Love.

This of course could have been a bunch of bull concocted by Kurt when put on the spot by the police. But then again - as some would later consider - perhaps Kurt really was afraid of his wife. He was genuinely hiding from her? Did Kurt actually lock himself in a room to hide from an out-of-control, rampaging Courtney Love? Only for her to call the police and report that he was suicidal?

If so, then this was a rather deceptive ploy on Courtney Love's part. How many spouses abuse their partner and then call the police on the one they just abused? She scared Kurt so badly he was hiding in a bathroom. Only for her to turn around and *call the cops on him*. If that is indeed what truly happened, Courtney would definitely take the cake for duplicity.

At any rate, Love expressed concern and the police took away some pills and Kurt's guns just to make sure. It's hard telling if the first responders were really all that concerned for Kurt or not. Maybe they were - but they also had to cover their bases. They knew that if something went wrong after they have left, they would be held responsible. For if they had done nothing and Kurt turned up dead the next day, there probably would have been a public outcry and they would have been to blame.

So for good measure, they did indeed attempt to suicide-proof the home, just in case. Courtney, in the meantime, staged a sort of impromptu intervention on 25 March 1994. She gathered together many musicians, record industry personnel (the aforementioned Danny Goldberg included), and friends of the troubled Kurt Cobain, in an effort to convince him to get off drugs and straighten up his life.

Kurt initially didn't appreciate the effort in the least and proceeded to ridicule all of them before running up to his room.

However, Kurt must have realized he was being a tad overdone (even a bit childish some might say?) and ultimately changed his mind. He agreed to the intervention and headed for a rehab clinic in LA. He showed up at the "Exodus Recovery Center" in Los Angeles on 30 March 1994.

According to the staff, Cobain was an ideal patient and didn't cause them any problems. He was pleasant and participated in counseling. But Cobain was planning a breakout. He actually scaled a fence and left the facility. He then hopped into a cab and showed up at the airport in LA from where he booked a plane to Seattle.

During the flight, he supposedly sat next to Duff McKagan from Guns N' Roses. McKagan was a bit wary of Kurt, since Kurt had in the past expressed animosity towards Roses' front man Axle Rose. Yet McKagan would later recall that Kurt seemed strangely happy to see him.

This was indeed really odd and almost comical considering the great animosity between Guns N' Roses and Nirvana at the time. Just a couple of years prior, Kurt and Krist apparently almost got into an all-out fist fight with Axl Rose and Duff McKagan. This was relayed by Kurt and Krist themselves at a benefit concert for LGBT rights. The concert was meant to raise awareness of proposed legislation in Oregon— - Oregon Ballot Measure 9 - which was viewed as being oppressive to the LGBT community.

At the time, Kurt Cobain and Axl Rose appeared to be complete opposites in this regard since Kurt had come out as openly supportive of LGBT rights whereas Axl Rose had made remarks and even penned song lyrics that many felt were homophobic. It was at the end of the concert that Kurt Cobain and his bass player Krist Novoselic recounted their run-in with Axl and Duff.

Kurt claimed that the incident happened at the MTV Music Awards. According to him, he and his bandmates, Courtney and the rest of their entourage were hanging out when Axl Rose and company walked by. According to him, he was holding his and Courtney's newborn child, Francis Bean, when he spontaneously shouted, "Hey Axl, will you be the godfather of our child?"

Now, one must really take Kurt's account with a big grain of salt. The two were already antagonists at that point, and here he's claiming that he was just minding his own business, and upon seeing Axl Rose, wanted to kindly request Axl to be the godfather of his child. Axl, and just about anyone else in earshot, would have clearly understood the mockery of the remarks.

It's hard telling what would have happened if Axl Rose didn't take the bait and instead cheerfully grinned, "Why certainly Mr. Kurt Cobain! Thank you for considering me for such a great honor! I would be more than happy to be your child's godfather!" If he had, Kurt and Courtney certainly would have had a good laugh at Axl's expense, even as they continued to make fun of the guy behind his back.

In reality, of course, the Cobains were not merely being friendly in their shouted remarks to Axl. Anyone who gives it some thought realizes that they were obviously attempting to provoke a response from him. They wanted him to react - and they wanted him to react badly. They saw the Guns N' Roses singer and proceeded to target him. In other words—*they were picking on him*.

As many who have researched the life of Kurt Cobain have come to realize - as much as Kurt might have been previously picked on in the past and as much as he typically presented himself as a victim, he himself had a tendency to belittle, demean and bully others. And considering how much of a loose cannon someone like Axl Rose could be, it's really not surprising that he went off when provoked.

At any rate, according to Kurt's account of that evening: Axl being Axl, immediately threatened to "take [him] down to the pavement if he didn't keep his, *as well as his* wife's mouth shut." After Kurt relayed these events to the crowd in the audience, Kurt's bassist Krist Novoselic chimed in: "True story. You heard it here first. And then I ran into Duff McKagan and that guy wanted to fight me and he had three bodyguards who were like pushing me around."

If any of this really happened as Kurt and Krist described, it really is comical to think that Kurt would end up seated next to the very same Duff McKagan on a plane a short time later. Forgetting all about any previous difficulties, Duff would later claim that Kurt was downright friendly. Even so, McKagan felt that something was odd about the whole thing.

On That Day

Upon his return to Seattle, for much of the first week of April, Cobain's whereabouts were entirely unknown. Love finally lost patience waiting and on 3 April hired a private investigator to find her husband. A few days later, on 8 April, Kurt Cobain was discovered at a house he owned on Lake Washington Boulevard. He was no longer among the living. He was in fact quite dead. He had been shot - from what was considered a self-inflicted gunshot wound. Nearby was a suicide note.

In the End

The note found next to Kurt's body seemed to be a clear indication that this was what he wanted. The supposed suicide note mentioned that he was simply tired of life in so many different ways, and wanted to take his exit from this world. However, there are those who believe that the suicide note was either forged or that it was a note from a previous diary entry that was being taken completely out of context.

The note read in part:

To Boddah,

Speaking from the tongue of an experienced simpleton who obviously would rather be an emasculated, infantile complain-ee. This note should be pretty easy to understand.

All the warnings from the punk rock 101 courses over the years, since my first introduction to the, shall we say, ethics involved with independence and the embracement of your community has proven to be very true. I haven't felt the excitement of listening to as well as creating music along with reading and writing for too many years now. I feel guilty beyond words about these things.

For example, when we're back stage and the lights go out and the manic roar of the crowds begins, it doesn't affect me the way in which it did for Freddie Mercury, who seemed to love and relish in the love and adoration from the crowd which is something I totally admire and envy. The fact is, I can't fool you, any one of you. It simply isn't fair to you or me. The worst crime I can think of would be to rip people off by faking it and pretending as if I'm having 100% fun. Sometimes I feel as if I should have a punch-in time clock before I walk out on stage. I've tried everything within my power to appreciate it (and I do, God, believe me, I do, but it's not enough). I appreciate the fact that I and we have affected and entertained a lot of people. It must be one of those narcissists who only appreciate things when they're gone. I'm too sensitive. I need to be slightly numb in order to regain the enthusiasm I once had as a child.

It would be a bit much to reproduce Kurt's note in full, but the first few paragraphs essentially convey the overall tone of his letter. The theme here is that Kurt was simply burned out with his music, his art, and life in general. He had lost the passion he once had and had essentially lost the will to live. The words here certainly do sound like a suicide note. But what if someone forged it?

Well, the very first line of the note carries a good argument against that theory. The first line reads "To Boddah." Many have mistaken this to be a misspelling of "Buddha" since Kurt had long been interested in Buddhism. But it's not. Boddah was actually an imaginary friend that Kurt had as a kid.

He once described Boddah in detail to his parents, stating that he was an alien from another planet that frequently visited him and told him stories. His parents laughed and shrugged off the whole thing at the time, but they didn't forget about it. And as soon as Kurt's mom, Wendy, saw the mention of Boddah, the memories came flooding back and she informed everyone else who this "Boddah" really was, and what he had meant to Kurt.

Since no one else knew anything about this Boddah character, this seems to indicate that only Kurt could have written at least part of the note. But what about the rest? There has long been a serious argument that Kurt did write much of the first half of the note, and that it was actually a letter explaining his decision to quit Nirvana - and that someone else altered the ending to make it appear more like a suicide note.

Such a thing wouldn't be too hard to imagine. Much of the context of the first half of the note does indeed deal with Kurt's increasing disenchantment with the band and the stage. In some ways, the note seems like a depressing journal entry, ripped out of Kurt's personal diary. Which with a little fine-tuning was made to look like a suicide note. But would someone really be nefarious enough to do such a thing? Did someone kill Kurt and simply made it look like a suicide? Perhaps we will never know.

Divya Bharti—Falling from the Heights of Bollywood

Who: Divya Bharti
Where: Mumbai, India
When: April 1993
Suspects: Herself - None
Conviction: None

Background Information

Even though she was only 19 years old when she suddenly passed away on 5 April 1993, Divya Bharti was already a rising star in her native India. She first emerged on the Bollywood (India's version of Hollywood) scene in 1990, by appearing in a much-loved film called "Bobbili Raja." This film was particularly popular in the regions of southern India, where Divya was already considered a celebrity.

It was after this success that she tried her luck in the so-called "Hindi" film market in northern India, with the release of her 1992 follow-up "Vishwatma." She was much applauded for her performance in this film, and in particular gained high praise for her rendition of a popular tune in India, called "Saat Samundar Paar."

On the heels of all of this, Divya Bharti found herself starring in yet another box office smash—*Pehlaj Nihlani Shola Aur Shabnam.* That's certainly a mouthful for non-Hindi speakers, but for those that are getting lost in translation here, just know that this movie was an immediate hit. She then followed up this blockbuster by starring in a romantic piece called "Deewana."

This film was also a blockbuster hit. But before the end of the year, her string of luck ended however when she starred in the box office flop *Hema Malini's Dil Asshna Hai.* In this piece, Divya portrayed a girl who worked as a dancer at a nightclub. In between her dance routines, she was obsessed with finding her long-lost mother. If the plot elements of an exotic dancer looking for her long-lost mom seem odd to you, you're not the only one.

Needless to say, this film fell flat with viewers and was an utter failure. Although it was a disappointment and a minor setback for Diywa, it most certainly wasn't the end of the world. Acting has its ups and downs after all. And even though this film was a box office blunder, there were certainly still plenty of possibilities for her to star in more successful films in the future. She was young and talented with plenty of potentials. So as depressing as this minor setback might have been at the time, it certainly wasn't reason enough to jump off a balcony, that's for sure!

Divya in the meantime, was moving on with her personal life. She married a guy by the name of Sajid Nadiawala on 20 May 1992. Not a lot is known about the exact details of their courtship, but it appears to have been a rather rapid one. They were initially quite happy together, although there are reports that Divya had suspicions that her husband might not always have been faithful to her. At any rate, the couple hadn't even been married a year when Divya suddenly passed away on 5 April 1993.

On That Day

Her death in itself is so puzzling and perplexing, no one seems to know for sure if it was a suicide, a murder, or just a tragic, freak accident. Divya was simply at home at her apartment in Mumbai, when she apparently fell right over the balcony of her high-rise. Of course, accidents happen all the time, and it could indeed be that she accidentally died this way.

But there are some complicating factors involved in this starlet's death. She had previously stated that she was depressed, and had ingested quite a few drinks just prior to her demise. She was picked up off the sidewalk where she had fallen, and taken to the hospital, but it was all in vain as she was quite clearly deceased.

The Suspects

Upon the death of this beautiful, young Bollywood actress, quite a bit of finger-pointing ensued. Her father was on the scene and is said to have been at his wit's end. He was heard ranting and raving about how someone had killed his daughter, and how he would give everything just to have her back.

His exact words in fact were, "They have killed my daughter. Burn down everything. I don't want anything, just give me back Divya." What was this all about? Was it the sad and devastated words of a parent who had just lost his child - or something more?

And while Divya's father seemed to be suggesting that his daughter had been the victim of foul play, her distraught brother seemed to suggest that it was suicide. For he was heard shouting, "I shouldn't have left my loving sister behind. I was with her till ten minutes before she could jump down. She was very depressed, she told me that. But, I didn't know she would do such a thing. I don't want anything. I just want my sister back. She was just nineteen. Is that the age to die?"

Her mother had perhaps the strangest reaction. Rather than being overcome with emotion, she was downright stoic. It's said that she quietly walked up to Divya's body, and pulled off the cover that had been draped over her, before placing her own head on Divya's heart. She silently stayed in this position for a moment, before she got up and walked away without uttering a word.

Divya's husband, Sajid, had a dramatic reaction all of his own when he was brought in to see his deceased wife. It's said that he actually fell down and suffered a heart attack, having to be admitted to a critical care unit himself. He was obviously shocked and in deep distress. There is no denying that. So, what happened to this promising star of Bollywood? Why did she fall from the heights of fame to oblivion down below?

Bobbi Kristina Brown
Did She Really Drown?

Who*:* Bobbi Kristina Brown
Where: Atlanta, Georgia
When: July 2015
Suspects*:* Nick Gordon
Conviction*:* None - Suspect Deceased

Background Information

Born on 4 March 1993 to superstar mother Whitney Houston and bad boy soul singer Bobby Brown, Bobbi Kristina Brown was literally born in the spotlight. Her parents' marriage was troubling from the start and continued to be tense and entirely tabloid provoking as Bobbi Kristina grew up. She even starred in a reality TV series about her family called "Being Bobby Brown (as in her father *Bobby Brown*)."

Nevertheless, she was close to both her parents, but especially to her mom. Her mother, Whitney, was a superstar and was never too far from a microphone - she likely hoped that perhaps Bobbi might even follow in her footsteps. After her mother's death in 2012, such a dream seemed less likely to come to fruition. Whitney Houston, who was 48 at the time, was found dead on 12 February 2012.

She apparently overdosed on drugs and drowned in a bathtub. Initially Brown did indicate some interest in picking up where her mother left off. That March, the then-teenaged Brown conducted an interview in which she stated that she did indeed intend to do the "singing thing." She also indicated an interest in an acting career, which showed some promise, as she played a receptionist in the Tyler Perry series, *For Better or Worse.*

But after Brown failed to get the role in a biographical film about her mother, called "Whitney", she became rather downcast and presumably gave up on acting altogether. Instead, she seemed to be ready to focus on her personal life. In July 2013 she publicly announced her intention of marrying Nick Gordon. This generated some blowback from friends and family alike since Gordon had been raised almost like an adopted son by the Houstons.

In fact, prior to the engagement, Bobbi herself had referred to him as her big brother. This of course raised some eyebrows, but it must be remembered that despite their close proximity growing up, they were not actually relatives, and such a romance between Bobbi and what was essentially a close family friend was not something unheard of.

Strangely enough, although the two never got married, Brown declared that they did, and set their wedding date as 9 January 2014. Roughly a year later, Bobbi Kristina was found unresponsive in a bathtub.

On That Day

The incident that ultimately led to Bobbi Kristina Brown's death, occurred on 31 January 2015. According to the official narrative, the only reason anyone was alerted to her distress, was that she had made a previous service call to the cable company.

The doorbell rang, and a house guest answered the door. It was the cable guy asking for his customer, Bobbi Kristina. The house guest then went off looking for her and discovered her face down in a bathtub. The house guest grabbed Bobbi's supposed husband, Nick Gordon.

The two men then frantically pulled Bobbi out of the tub and tried to give her CPR. The paramedics were also summoned, and Bobbi was taken to the hospital. Meanwhile, Bobbi Kristina's father, Bobby Brown, was flown in from Los Angeles to Atlanta, Georgia to be at his daughter's side. It's said that during her time in the hospital, he watched her like a hawk, and was especially wary of her supposed husband, Nick Gordon.

The word "supposed" must be used repeatedly, since the wedding was never officially recognized. In fact, Bobbi Kristina's dad, Bobby Brown, didn't recognize it and made a point during his daughter's stay at the hospital to take note of this fact. He actually had his lawyer tell the press unequivocally, "Bobbi Kristina is not and has never been married to Nick Gordon."

Strangely enough, she was apparently the victim of a drug overdose, drowning in a tub, just like her mother in 2012. Unlike her mother, Whitney, Bobbi was revived but was found to be brain dead. After being in hospice care until July of that year, she was pronounced dead on the 26th of that month. She was only 22 years old.

The Suspect

After Bobbi Kristina Brown's death, Nick Gordon would continue to cause controversy and suspicion. In 2015 he appeared on a Dr. Phil show, in which he was grilled (although somewhat half-heartedly) by Dr. Phil about what had happened to Bobbi Kristina. During the course of the interview, Gordon, who answered questions while sitting next to his mother, acted truly bizarrely.

At one point, a clearly frustrated Dr. Phil told Gordon he needed to "man up", which only seemed to infuriate Gordon. His mother, in fact, had to step in and soothe Nick's nerves as she chided, "Respect him [Dr. Phil]. Respect him."

Nick, despite all his fury, was still doing damage control and lashing out at a popular TV show host, which obviously wasn't going to do him much good. Around this time Gordon was hit with a wrongful death suit, and ordered to pay out $36 million. Mr. Gordon clearly seemed to be spiraling out of control and he wouldn't live much longer after this ruling.

In The End

In fact, Nick Gordon passed away on 1 January 2020. It was right at the dawning of a new and troubled decade that Nick Gordon made his exit. So, what happened? Did Bobbi Kristina really just drown? Or was Nick Gordon somehow responsible for her "wrongful death" as the civil suit claimed? Only Nick Gordon might know for sure. And it seems that whatever secrets he may have had in regard to Bobbi Kristina's death, he chose to take them with him to the grave.

Taking a Second Glance at the Killing of Jack Nance

Who*:* Jack Nance
Where: Hollywood, California
When: December 1996
Suspects*:* Unknown
Conviction*:* None

Background Information

Jack Nance hailed from Dallas, Texas, but spent much of his life in Hollywood. He was a famous actor celebrated for many classic roles. He was particularly known for the iconic part he played in the 1978 film "Eraserhead", an avant-garde horror flick that has since gained quite a cult following. He was also known for his contribution to the 1980s Science Fiction hit "Dune." His latest claim to fame, however, was when he starred in the David Lynch series "Twin Peaks."

Here he played the part of a hard-nosed lumber mill foreman named Pete Martell. Pete was a typical rough and tumble tough guy who didn't mess around. No one wanted to upset Pete Martell. But what about Jack Nance? Jack was 53 years old when he paid a visit to a local LA donut shop in December 1996, only to have a run-in with his killers. He was apparently just out to get some donuts early that morning when some guys started giving him a hard time.

Jack - despite any risk that might be involved - was not known to back down from anyone. And he most likely gave these tough guys a piece of his mind. He called them a bunch of bums and said they needed to go out "get a haircut" and "get a job." The haircut remark can be construed as being oddly ironic since Jack is remembered for his Eraserhead role in which he sported hair that stood about six inches high!

At any rate, whatever Jack's challenge to the young men was, they answered back with their fists. And apparently gave Mr. Nance a pretty severe beating. Nevertheless, he managed to dust himself off and got his donuts and himself home.

It's perhaps also worth mentioning that Jack Nance was completely drunk at the time. He was known to put a few drinks away, and he was apparently pretty well-lit when he made his way down to this local donut shop. He no doubt wanted to put a few good pastries in his alcohol-filled stomach to soak up all the booze. Unfortunately, when Jack Nance drank, his mouth became entirely unfiltered.

We've all seen drunks who hit the booze and then mouth off to just about anyone for just about any reason - and apparently, this was the sort of state that Jack was in. We can just imagine him stumbling into the shop to get his donuts, mumbling to himself, obviously inebriated. Perhaps the two young guys who hassled him made a comment to that effect.

It doesn't seem that they realized Jack was a famous actor. They probably didn't recognize him for his role as Pete Martel in Twin Peaks. It seems that to them, Jack was just some drunk old man who had wandered the streets. Maybe they commented as such. One could imagine them pouting and laughing as Jack stumbled across the donut shop with his pastries in hand. Maybe one of them shouted, "Ha! Look at that old drunk!"

Perhaps this was all it took for Jack to turn around and snarl, "Hey you bums! Why don't you get a haircut and a job? Good for nothing creeps!" The intensity and the hostility that Jack Nance dished out were probably too much for these hoodlums to ignore. And what they might have otherwise laughed off as a funny drunk, presented an immediate challenge to them.

This is likely what led to the sudden eruption of violence. And although Jack's mouth was ready to do battle, unfortunately, his thin, weak frame was not! And the awful bruises he left that donut shop adorned with, testified to that fact. The pummeled Jack Nance had been rendered into a walking set of bruises.

On 29 December, he even managed to meet up with some friends, Leo Bulgarini and Catherine Case, for a meal. The friends were glad to see Jack, but they couldn't help but notice the bruises and black eye he still sported from the previous incident. They of course asked him what was wrong, and he informed them of how he had just gotten into a fight with some guys at a local donut shop. The incident seemed terrible to all involved since Jack was quite frail at this point, and certainly not in any condition to sustain major blows to the head.

Nevertheless, despite a complaint of having a "bad headache", Jack promptly assured everyone he was fine. Unfortunately, he was not, but no one involved knew he was suffering from internal bleeding. It was this internal flow of blood dislodged by his assailants, that would ultimately do him in, and he died shortly thereafter.

On That Day

On 30 December 1996, the day after the incident, he was found dead by his buddy Leo, who just so happened to stop by. He was discovered laying "facedown" in his bathroom. That headache apparently got considerably worse in the interim. It was later determined that Jack had perished as a result of an unchecked "subdural hematoma." In other words, he succumbed to all of that internal bleeding that the pounding of several fists to his head had induced.

The Suspects

To this day, his assailants - and ultimately his killers - have never been found. In the meantime, there are those who have speculated that perhaps his killing was not as random as it might seem. Some have wondered if perhaps Jack was purposefully targeted.

A highly controversial conspiracy theorist by the name of Michael J. Anderson infamously went so far as to accuse filmmaker David Lynch of having somehow been behind the hit. This is a bridge too far for most - but still. This strange case still has plenty of questions that remain entirely unanswered.

John Lennon's
Secret Admirer

Who*:* John Lennon
Where: New York, New York
When: December 1980
Suspects*:* Mark David Chapman
Conviction*:* 1981

Background Information

In the 1970s, John Lennon left the Beatles and embarked upon a solo career. This new path yielded much fruit as it pertains to further hit songs, rendering such mainstays as "Happy Xmas," "Imagine," "Nobody Told Me," "Instant Karma" and more. In the meantime, the former Liverpool, England resident moved into the prestigious Dakota Apartment complex in New York, New York.

Lennon, although obviously quite famous, neither kept a low profile nor had much in the way of security. In fact, when he was killed, all his murderer had to do was walk right up to him. On 8 December 1980, after John Lennon's car rolled up to the Dakota building, a deranged fan - Mark David Chapman - who had been following the movements of Lennon for some time, watched as John and his wife, Yoko Ono, got out of the car, and headed toward the apartment building where they lived.

The 31-year-old Chapman, as if he were the building nightwatchman, positioned himself right at the door and was standing there as the couple strode up to him. But this man, who was carrying a .38 revolver, was not there to protect the couple that evening - he was there to hurt them. *At least one of them.*

It's somewhat ironic that Mark David Chapman was almost posing as a security guard at the doors of the Dakota, since in his troubled life, working as an armed guard had been one of his mainstays. Mark hailed from Georgia, where he was a good student and initially seemed to have a promising career as a counselor. He in fact worked as one at the YMCA before losing the job and settling for a gig as a security guard in Atlanta.

Apparently unable to find any other type of work, he seemingly embraced this lot in life, even going further by getting licensed to carry a gun. But Mark was presumably stuck in a depressing rut. So much so that in 1977, he attempted to take his own life. He was on vacation in Hawaii when he tried to commit suicide. He got into a rental car, hooked up a hose to the exhaust, put the tube in the window, rolled it up, started the engine, and waited for death.

But before the carbon monoxide could get to him, a local fisherman rescued him - saving his life. That may have been good for Mark, but unbeknownst to anyone at the time, ultimately bad for John Lennon. For even while Mark swears off the notion of suicide, it wouldn't be long before his dark and troubled thoughts turned to murder instead. In the meantime, he met a 26-year-old travel agent by the name of "Gloria."

The two hit it off and got married in the summer of 1978. Mark in the meantime, began to develop his rather unhealthy obsession with John Lennon. He supposedly started out as an admirer of Lennon and his music group. But somewhere along the way, his admiration turned into a strange and unreasoning hatred.

Although the Beatles broke up several years prior, for Mark David Chapman it was almost like it was just yesterday. He blamed Lennon not only for the breakup but for a whole host of problems in the world and even in his own personal life.

For some bizarre, entirely irrational reason, he made John Lennon the sole focal point of all of his many points of rage. Gloria was privy to his many rambles about his hatred for the former Beatle, and when she learned that he was planning a trip to New York to pay Lennon a visit, she was deeply concerned. The first time Mark headed off to New York, however, he apparently had a change of heart and came back to his worried wife.

She was relieved and hoped that he had put Lennon out of his mind for good. But little did she know that this first trip to New York was merely a scouting mission - a dry run if you will - for the diabolical murder he was developing in the dark recesses of his mind. Mark David Chapman soon informed his wife that he was returning to New York. He assured her that it had nothing at all to do with John Lennon, but merely to check out some "work opportunities."

Mark, however, had a narrow focus on Lennon all along. He arrived in NYC in 1980, ready and willing to engage in murderous mayhem. And as soon as he arrived, he leased the closest flat to Lennon's place that he could find. He then took a copy of Lennon's latest album—*Double Fantasy*—and walked right up to the door of Lennon's apartment building and simply waited for the star to arrive.

John Lennon was a no-show on this particular day, so Mark had to give up and go back to his flat, his murderous impulses unfulfilled. The next day he got up bright and early. The first thing he did was head over to a bookstore where he bought a copy of the classic novel, "The Catcher in the Rye." He then went right back to Lennon's apartment, where, like the hardcore stalker he was, he waited, waited, and waited, for Lennon to return.

That afternoon he sat and kept a close watch as John's then 5-year-old boy, Sean Lennon, arrived on the scene with his nanny. Little Sean was there - but still no John. Mark David Chapman nevertheless waited, and sure enough, John and Yoko arrived at the apartment building fresh from an interview they had just conducted at the local radio station, RKO Radio.

Mark walked right up to John with the album *Double Fantasy* in hand and asked him to sign it. Perhaps Mark in his twisted mind had told himself that if John was snooty, uptight, and refused to give him an autograph, he would just shoot him in return. As if such a refusal would have given him a reason to pull out his gun and commit murder. But if that was indeed what Mark intended, John Lennon did not fall into this trap.

In fact, John was downright kind, courteous, and well-mannered. He readily replied "Sure" and in a show of compassion and concern for the stranger at his door, even asked Mark if he wanted or needed anything else. Mark, seeming almost disappointed in John's courteousness, simply muttered "Thanks a lot."

John and Yoko then left again, and Mark had to consider the implications of what he had observed. In his mind, Mark had turned Lennon into a demonic, arrogant fiend, who needed to be destroyed. But now that he had met him, he was just a "regular guy." Even a fairly nice and decent guy, who had taken some time out of his busy schedule to give him an autograph and wish him well.

John was not the monster he had imagined. Now, what was he to do? Just shake off his mad quest and go home? History certainly would have been a lot different (a lot better, with full-blown Beatles reunions no doubt) if he had done so. But unfortunately, this was simply not the case. No, instead, Mark

David Chapman thought about it for a moment and decided that even if John was a nice guy, he still needed to complete his deadly mission.

On That Day

He continued to loiter around Lennon's apartment building and even managed to strike up a conversation with the guy who guarded the door - the real security guard, Jose Perdomo. Amazingly, Mark hung around all the way until 11 pm when Yoko and John both arrived back at the apartment building. Mark would later claim that he felt absolutely compelled to take action at this point—as if this was his chance and the monsters inside his head demanded that he seize the opportunity.

While he was a short distance away, he watched Lennon accompany Yoko to the door of the apartment building and decided to act. He stepped forward and opened fire, hitting John Lennon multiple times in the back. The doorman immediately went into action and lunged for Mark's wrist, and with an expert twisting motion, he was able to let Mark lose his grip on the gun.

The guard then tackled Mark and made sure he was not able to do anyone else any more harm. The doorman, who knew John and Yoko on a personal level, was beside himself with grief. It is said that he screamed, "What did you do? What have you done?" As John lay dying, Mark then supposedly apologized, "I'm sorry."

But for some reason, murderer Mark David Chapman, just couldn't seem to help himself. And after he was in custody, he admitted that a large part of his mischief wasn't solely about John Lennon, but that he considered targeting other famous people as well. It seems Mark primarily wanted to strike out at someone who was a celebrity.

This miserable man who felt so inadequate with himself wanted what he perceived as a big target to dispense his rage on. He wanted to reach out and strike someone who was up high so that he could bring that person down as low as he felt. Ultimately, Lennon, who notoriously disliked security, was simply much easier for Chapman to reach than many other superstars might have been.

If only Lennon had some extra security around him that day, perhaps he would have been spared. One can only imagine how many more songs and albums Lennon might have composed. Perhaps even a Beatles reunion concert would have been in the works. But sadly, Mark David Chapman made sure none of that would ever happen.

The Suspect

Mark, of course, was the prime and only suspect in this case, and was immediately taken into custody. He always openly admitted to the killing. It would have been quite difficult for him to do anything otherwise, considering the circumstances. He was seen shooting Lennon right out in the open by several witnesses and was arrested right there on the scene. Nevertheless, there was some pushback by his legal defense, who wished for him to plead not guilty by reason of insanity.

In The End

Chapman steadfastly refused and insisted that he enter a plea of guilty. His wishes were granted and he was found guilty as charged. On 24 August 1981, he was sentenced to serve "20 years to life" in prison. This means that although he was not guaranteed parole after serving 20 years, he would have hearings for the rest of his life until he was either paroled or died in prison. As of this writing, at the many parole hearings he attended, no one has yet dared indulge Mark David Chapman any opportunity for parole.

NFL Star Sean Taylor's Shocking Murder

Who*:* Sean Taylor
Where: Hollywood, California
When: November 2007
Suspects*:* Venjah K Hunte, Eric Rivera, Jason Scott Mitchell, Charles Kendrick Lee Wardlow, Eric Rivera
Conviction*:* 2008

Background Information

The NFL can be a rough place - but nevertheless, Sean Taylor was someone who certainly had a lot of promise. He was a rising star who played for the Washington Redskins. Taylor had been recruited to the team as a "first-round pick" during the NFL draft in 2004. He was a popular player, and was humorously nicknamed the "Meast." Since he was said to be "half man, half beast" regarding his powerful exploits on the field.

Unfortunately, that promise was cut short. In November 2007, his house in Fort Myers, Florida, was invaded by a bunch of crooks, trying to steal. Sean lived in a lovely neighborhood and his extravagant house was most certainly a tempting target for any would-be thieve. At the time, Sean was home with his girlfriend, Jackie Garcia Hayley, and their 18-month-old daughter.

Everyone in the home was sound asleep when a disturbance was heard around one in the morning. Sean, as any guy in this position might do, wanted to protect his loved ones. He actually instructed his girlfriend to hide under the covers with the baby, while he checked out the sound. He picked up a machete he had on hand for exactly such a purpose, went out of the bedroom, and shut the door behind him.

Sean Taylor confronted the intruders and was shot in the leg. His girlfriend, Jackie, didn't quite know what was happening, but would later recall "a lot of noise" and "commotion" took place. She then saw the door to the bedroom was open. She no doubt was fearful that it was the intruders coming for her, but the person standing in the doorway was her husband, shot and bleeding. Without even taking a single item - after the havoc, they wreaked - the cowardly intruders fled the scene.

On That Day

Initially, it was expected that Sean would live, but it seems that the bullet fired by these crooks managed to cut off a major artery in his leg. The severing of this artery caused Taylor to bleed to death. He was taken to the hospital, but he had already lost too much blood and passed away shortly thereafter. Sean's dad, Pero, was the one who broke the news.

Pedro Taylor announced, "It is with deep regret that a young man had to come to his end so soon. Many of his fans loved him because of the way he played football. Many of his opponents feared him, of the way he approached the game. Others misunderstood him, many appreciated him and his family loved him. I can only hope and pray that Sean's life was not in vain, that it might touch others in a special way."

The Investigation

Immediately after his demise, the investigation as to who was behind this crime was underway. It was soon learned that the intruders who had barged into his home that day were four guys: Venjah K Hunte, Eric Rivera, Jason Scott Mitchell, and Charles Kendrick Lee Wardlow. All four were charged with second-degree murder, armed burglary, and home invasion.

In May 2008, another assailant was taken into custody., This man was really only a 16-year-old kid at the time of the assault. Despite his youth, he was tried as an adult, and he too was charged with murder. It was ultimately discovered that Eric Rivera was the one who fired the shot that ended Sean Taylor's life.

For this offense, Rivera received 57 years in prison. Some have since wondered if the killing was not as random as it first seemed. Was this really a so-called robbery gone bad? Or was there something more at work? Was Sean targeted by someone? Taylor's own personal attorney, Richard Sharpstein, weighed in on this matter but was ultimately unconvinced. He would later state, "My instincts tell me this was not a murder or a hit. It was certainly not professionally done since two random shots were fired."

Even so, there are some things about this case that really makes one wonder. Most startling is the fact that Sean's home had already been broken into just a week before he was killed. When no one was home, someone had climbed in through a window and ransacked the place. But yet again, even though someone was rummaging through everything, nothing was taken. This is definitely not the normal behavior of would-be robbers.

Even more bizarre, whoever broke in - rather than taking things - *actually left something.* They left a knife, strangely positioned and placed on Sean's bed. Was this a warning? Or an indication of things to come? We can only guess. And in particular, we can only wonder if Sean Taylor had any enemies that had it out for him. According to a police report from 2005, —he might have had them after all.

In 2005, Taylor himself was arrested for supposedly pointing a gun at a group of people whom he accused of stealing one of his "all-terrain vehicles." He would ultimately plead no contest, to have the matter quietly dropped. Even so, one of the men Taylor waved that gun at - Ryan Hill - was apparently not quite ready to forget about the incident. And actually filed a lawsuit against him.

In The End

Even so, Ryan Hill has long denied playing any role in Sean Taylor's death. It would indeed seem to defy logic, since why would he want a man dead whom he was actively trying to get money out of by way of a lawsuit? He needed Taylor alive to get money out of him - *not dead.* Much about this case still remains a mystery.

Jam Master Jay's Killer Gets Away

Who: Jam Master Jay
Where: Queens, New York, New York
When: October 2002
Suspects: Karl Jordan Jr. and Ronald Washington
Conviction: Pending

Background Information

Jason Mizell, also known as "Jam Master Jay", grew up in Hollis, Queens, in New York City. Hollis is a poorer section of Queens - yet still much better than many other neighborhoods in NYC. Jason himself was surrounded by relative signs of affluence, but he didn't have to go far to find those who had much less.

It was just a hop, skip, and jump from his neighborhood to nearby Jamaica, Queens, where poverty, crime, as well as a rich culture, and music, were overflowing. Jason spent most of his teenage years in both Jamaica and Hollis. This was his old stomping grounds where he first honed his chops as a DJ

He was just 16 years old when he regularly began DJing and partying at "Dorian's", a well-known establishment in Hollis. As his acclaim grew for being able to spin great beats, so did the crowds. Often the building itself became so crowded, that concert goers "spilled out into the street."

During these concerts, random rappers would often rap over the records that Jay spun. Eventually taking the guest spots were his buddies, Joseph "Run" Simmons, and Darryl "DMC" McDaniels. It was after the vocals of Run and DMC were incorporated with Jam Master Jay's beats that the hip hop group the world would come to know and love as *Run DMC* was born.

On That Day

Hollis, Queens was where it all started, and coincidentally enough, it was also in Hollis that both Jam Master Jay (and by extension Run DMC) would meet their end. For on 30 October 2002, while sitting in a recording studio, Jam Master Jay was shot and killed

Jay was on a very tight schedule at the time of his death. He had just flown into New York, from Birmingham, Alabama, where this legendary celebrity disc jockey had been spinning records at a concert. Soon after he arrived back in NYC he was in the studio to put some finishing touches on a few recordings. Jam Master Jay, since leaving behind the glory days of Run DMC, had proved how versatile he was by branching out his artistic talent in multiple directions.

He was frequently collaborating with other local artists. Most notably, just prior to his demise, he had laid down some tracks for an up-and-coming rapper by the name of Curtis Jackson. Mr. Jackson is more widely recognized as the hip-hop powerhouse "50 Cent." Back in the Fall of 2002, 50 Cent was just on the verge of making it big time and it was industry connections with old pros like Jam Master Jay, which helped facilitate his rise.

At any rate, Jam Master Jay had a lot of work to do in the studio - but he also planned a lot of catching up with his family. And immediately afterward he wanted to head back to his own personal residence to catch up with his wife and kids. But sadly enough - Jam Master Jay's killers had different plans.

It's said that two men barged into his studio, put a gun to his head, and killed him on the spot. Jay didn't even have the chance to begin work on his recordings. It was around 7 pm, he had just arrived at the studio and his techs were prepping the boards. As was his custom, he kicked back and played some video games to unwind while he waited for the studio hands to finish their work so he could begin laying down tracks. Jay and a buddy of his were playing a football video game of some sort, staring up at the screen, when an intruder came in and shot Jay in the head.

The Suspects

Jam Master Jay's murder was clearly observed by several people. Police would later complain that although there were witnesses who could report every single detail of *how* Jam Master Jay was killed, they all stopped short of giving any details as to *who* the killers might have been.

It's been speculated that this was due to some sort of unspoken rule of the streets, that one should not snitch out the identity of someone else to the police. Also, it must be realized that for those who live in rough neighborhoods, sometimes ratting out criminals is easier said than done. This is due to the widespread prevalence of retaliation. Such things were no doubt on the minds of those stunned witnesses.

As much as they wanted to get justice for Jay, they also wanted to keep breathing. And there was likely a deep and heavy fear that if they said anything, they would be in the crosshairs of vengeful gangsters. As such, the strange, stony wall of silence around the identities of Jay's killers remained in place. In 2020 this wall finally began to crumble and the two main suspects in the killing were finally arrested.

It's alleged that Jay, who was on the hook for a $500,000 tax bill, had declined to pay an old "drug debt." Jay apparently feared the internal revenue service much more than he feared the drug dealers. The dealer, Curtis Scoon, nonetheless, was determined not to be ignored and ordered Karl Jordan Jr. and his accomplice Ronald Washington to storm into the studio to collect.

In The End

Yet rather than getting any money, they took Jay's life instead. As of this writing, a trial date is set for the two men later in 2023. In 2022, Karl was fighting the charges with his attorney claiming that authorities had violated due process by waiting too long. We'll just have to stay tuned to see what might happen next.

Sid and Nancy
The Romeo and Juliet of Punk?

Who: Nancy Spungen
Where: New York, New York
When: October 1978
Suspects: Sid Vicious
Conviction: Suspect deceased.

Background Information

Nancy Spungen was an American living in Britain when she hooked up with punk rocker Sid Vicious (real name John Simon Ritchie). She hailed from suburban Philadelphia, a far cry from the rough and tumble world she fell into. According to her mother, Deborah, Nancy was troubled almost from the beginning.

This isn't really an understatement, since Deborah would later recall Nancy as a baby screaming and crying and being entirely inconsolable. Deborah was a first-time mother - only 20 at the time herself - and began to think the child simply didn't like her. As the years passed, the situation didn't get much better. Growing up, Nancy became increasingly moody, disaffected, and agitated.

According to Deborah her daughter "wanted to die" since the age of eleven. Nancy's self-destructive death wish ultimately proved to be too much for the family to handle. By the time she was a teenager, she had become such a handful that her own mother had to put her out of the house, out of fear for her other two children. She began following various bands, and when the first wave of punk hit Britain, she booked a flight to London to go on tour with the music group—*The Heartbreakers*—in 1976.

Sidney Vicious was the bass player for the up-and-coming British punk rock band, called "The Sex Pistols." To say that The Sex

Pistols were *up-and-coming* is at risk of a severe understatement since many would argue that the Pistols were incredible pioneers, perhaps even the originators of punk music itself. Whatever the case may be, Johnny Rotten's over-the-top vocals and lyrics, and Sid Vicious's sneer were well-known in the world of punk rock by the time Nancy met Sid.

Sid, although credited on The Sex Pistols albums, was actually a latecomer to the band, arriving in early 1977. All of the most infamous of The Sex Pistols' songs, such as "Anarchy in the UK" and "God Save the Queen", had already been penned. The old bassist had been fired after laying down several recordings, and Sid was recruited as an afterthought, mainly because he was good friends with The Sex Pistols' front man Johnny Rotten.

Johnny Rotten and Sid Vicious grew up together and were in many ways kindred spirits. Initially, a great and formidable collaboration seemed to be in the works. Shortly after he joined the group, met Nancy Spungen. Nancy was known to hang around and follow bands of all sorts. She was indeed known for being a classic "groupie."

Upon meeting Sid, she immediately latched onto the young punk rocker, and soon the two were inseparable. Yet Nancy was the one who introduced Sid to many of her bad habits - including shooting up heroin. The two had a strange and dysfunctional relationship. They were known to alternate between shouting and slapping each other one moment, to being kind and loving with one another the next.

Sid was always there to comfort Nancy when she was going through withdrawal, but he was also the one to beat her if she didn't procure drugs, or if she didn't get money for some devious act he had pimped her out for. Nancy was also at times quite loving towards Sid, she was often seen preparing meals for him, even "cutting his meat."

Their relationship was certainly odd to outsiders, but as they say - love truly is in the eye of the beholder. At any rate, they apparently saw something in each other, and whatever it was,— outlasted the Pistols. The Sex Pistols ultimately broke up in 1978, and in the aftermath, Sid and Nancy headed off to America to pursue other interests.

It was in America that their drug habits, prospects, and the relationship took a turn for the worse. Strung out on drugs in the famed "Chelsea Hotel" in New York (checked in as Mr. and Mrs. John Simon Ritchie), without any hope of making more money, the two got into an argument.

On That Day

No one knows for sure exactly what happened, but in the early morning hours of the 12th October 1978, Nancy Spungen ended up with a knife in her stomach and bled to death.— She was only 20 years old. Sid didn't try to flee the scene and was found right there at Nancy's side, rambling and entirely incoherent.

The Suspect

This terrible sight was later reenacted in the movie "Sid and Nancy" in which actor Gary Oldman played the part of the incoherent, drugged-out Sid. In the film, Sid remains seated at the end of the bed in that dark hotel room, even as the police storm in. Oldman's Sid Vicious seems to be completely in another world, not even aware that Nancy is dead when the police demand to know what happened.

Considering how far gone, this just might be an accurate enough portrayal of Sid's mental state at the time. Nevertheless, upon being confronted by authorities he didn't seem to have anything to hide. In fact, he initially openly admitted to stabbing Nancy Spungen but later suggested that perhaps she had simply "fallen on the knife" instead.

There was always some speculation that perhaps Sid and Nancy entered into some sort of suicide pact, But Sid chickened out when it was his turn to die. This theory was explored in the aforementioned film, "Sid and Nancy." In the movie, just before she was killed, the actress who plays Nancy Spungen, shouts at Sid about some "promise" he had made about ending her life. Sid shouts, "You want to die? You want to die?" There's a tussle, and somehow or another, she gets stabbed in the stomach.

As portrayed in the film, it was as if Sid actually fulfilled Nancy's own death wish. Nancy was often suicidal, and the notion that she was nagging Sid to fulfill a promise - a suicide pact if you will - was explored in the making of the film. If this was indeed the case, it seems that Sid was probably meant to turn the knife on himself afterward, but simply didn't do it. Instead, he waited right there until the police arrived.

In The End

Sid Vicious was ushered off to New York's Rikers Island prison to have it all sorted out. He was able to post bond and was temporarily released. Yet, during this brief stint of freedom allotted to him, he was found dead from an apparent drug overdose. So ended the lives of these two star-crossed celebrities - the ill-fated Romeo and Juliet of punk rock.

Thomas Ince—Fortune and Fame Driven to the Brink

Who*:* Thomas Ince
Where: Hollywood, California
When: November 1924
Suspects*:* William Randolph Hearst - Unknown
Conviction*:* None

Background Information

The ill-fated Hollywood producer, Thomas Ince, was born in the year 1880, with bustling Rhode Island as his backdrop. He was raised much like a vagabond, moving from one place to another with his family of burgeoning performers. His mother and father were both comic performers who arrived from Britain, seeking to make it big in the Vaudeville circuit in the United States.

His dad was a comic who called himself "Pop" whereas his mother was a songstress who told jokes on the side. It's said that little Thomas joined the family trade at the ripe old age of six when he began to ham it up in front of audiences, along with his siblings. And by the time the budding performer was 15 years of age, he had begun performing with another eager entertainer— Ellinor "Nell" Kershaw.

Ellinor would go on to marry Thomas in the year 1907. It was when he was still in his 20s that Thomas began working for a production company called Biograph. During this stint, he took a strong interest in producing Western-themed films. He ultimately made his way out to California, where he and his wife Nell took up shop around Silver Lake. Eager to get started Thomas immediately began looking for a gig as a producer.

He was ultimately tapped by one Adolph Zukor to take part in the establishment of a new production company called Paramount Pictures. Paramount, of course, would in time, become quite famous. Back in the 1910s when Thomas was still cutting his teeth, however, there was no guarantee on how any of it might end up.

It was in July of 1915 that Thomas hooked up with the likes of Mack Sennett and D. W. Griffith, with whom he established Triangle Film Corporation. It was through this outfit, that the piece "Intolerance" was developed in 1916. This film was part of several that would come off the Thomas Ince assembly line, such as "Hell's Hinges" and "Civilization."

For it was Thomas Ince who began a meticulous process of streamlining the production of films. It was after he became quite successful at film-making, and the money came rolling in, that he squared away some 18,000 acres of land in California's Pacific Palisades, which he dubbed "Inceville."

Here at his own personal studio, he would crank out even more hits. By the 192os, Thomas Ince was indeed a wealthy man, who was quite well known in the industry. He then bought even more land for himself, this time in Beverly Hills, where he set down roots for his family. Ince would then forge Paramount Pictures with Adolph Zukor, before forging Thomas H. Ince Studios, were he would make movies such as "Human Wreckage" and "Anna Christie."

But these latest productions somehow fell flat and failed to make a stir, and by 1924, Ince was losing money. It's believed that it was his sudden financial downturn, which led him to partner with William Randolph Hearst. Hearst of course, was an extremely wealthy businessman, promoter, and publisher.

On That Day

It was while in discussions with Hearst as to how Ince could best reinvigorate his work, that Thomas Ince took a ride on the mogul's luxury yacht. It also happened to be Ince's 44th birthday. It's said that after hooking up with Hearst, Thomas Ince rang in his b-day in style, drinking a liberal amount of champagne and dining on "salted almonds" even though he was told to swear off such things do to a bad "peptic ulcer."

According to the official version of events, during that ill-fated birthday party on a boat—Thomas Ince suddenly doubled over in obvious distress. He was then sent home where he died the following day, November 19, 1924. In the aftermath, it has long been suspected that his death was somehow a homicide. But others have pointed out that Ince was a classic workaholic. He worked around the clock, barely got any rest, and had a terrible diet—could these factors have led to his demise?

In the End

Any sudden death on board a boat under uncertain circumstances is bound to cause suspicion. But the most shocking part of this story was that an erroneous (at least they say it was erroneous) newspaper story was released shortly after Mr. Ince's demise which unequivocally stated "Movie Producer Shot on Hearst Yacht." This headline was quickly retracted, but with very little explanation as to why someone would print such a thing at all—if it weren't true.

Interestingly enough, since William Randolph Hearst ran his own newspaper, it was under his direction that the official line about Thomas Ince suffering from the onset of a sudden illness became the story to hit the mainstream. Hearst early on, obviously realized that those who control the mainstream narrative—control a great deal of public perception. The exact cause of this Hollywood legend's death is still being discussed.

Busby Berkeley
Beats the Rap

Who*:* Busby Berkeley
Where: Hollywood, California
When: September 1935
Suspects*:* Busby Berkley
Conviction*:* None - Acquitted

Background and Information

Busby Berkeley—the name might not be immediately familiar to most, but he was a big deal in Hollywood for many decades. Busby Berkeley was a film producer and musical director, who had a hand in many epic Hollywood productions. He was also very nearly convicted of multiple manslaughter charges in the 1930s, due to the deaths of several, by way of his out-of-control vehicle.

Some would later argue that it was only through his fortune and fame that Busby Berkeley escaped serious punishment, while others would contend that the tragic accident was just that—*a tragic accident.* Berkeley a lifelong Los Angeles resident, did indeed have deep connections in the film industry. But prior to becoming a Hollywood kingpin, back in the 1920s, he had worked as a dance choreographer on Broadway.

Here he becomes known for directing chorus girls into tight "geometric patterns." Just think of a group of dancers such as the famed Rockettes, forming rings, triangles, and squares as they shimmy, dance, and kick their legs in the air—and you get the idea. His work gained attention, and he was soon recruited by film mogul Samuel Goldwyn to head to Hollywood, so he could work on musical numbers for the film. This would lead to Berkeley working on such productions as the 1932 epic "Night World."

Much of his work was filled with happy-go-lucky dance routines, but some of his pictures had a more serious element, such as his film "Gold Diggers," which had a musical number called "Remember My Forgotten Man." The song was about the terrible treatment of World War One veterans during the Great Depression. It's almost hard for us to fathom today since most of us are conditioned to honor and revere our veterans—but this was not always the case.

And immediately after World War One, the returning soldiers, with no jobs, and no massive government programs to help them along, were routinely discarded, rejected, and cast aside. And after the Great Depression set in, matters would only become much worse for these disillusioned veterans.

At one point, frustrated out of work World War One Veterans even marched on the capital in search of bonuses that they never received. The protesters who were dubbed the "bonus army" —instead of being listened to, were brutally driven from the streets by authorities.

They were indeed often cast aside and forgotten. And it was in Berkeley's day and age, this rare bit of remorse over how these veterans were treated was expressed in that tune "Remember My Forgotten Man."

It was a couple of years after this moving piece, however, that Berkeley would decide to drink and drive one fine night in September of 1935, and the results would not be good. Berkeley would get into an accident on the highway; it's said he abruptly changed lanes and hit another vehicle head-on.

On That Day

It all began at a festive Hollywood shindig that took place during the evening of September 8th, 1935. Busby Berkeley himself would be injured, and two others would lose their lives. The accident occurred while Busby was driving through the winding roads of Santa Monica Canyon. Busby was indeed buzzed, and he was driving much faster around those dangerous curves than he should.

He was making a rapid, tight turn, when his car suddenly fishtailed, and Busby lost all ability to steer his vehicle. It was at this precise moment that the tire on the front, the left side of his car went out. This blown tire sent him barreling into the other lane, and into the traffic on the other side. In a terrific crash, he ended up hitting another car head-on.

The blow of Busby's car was so forceful, it actually flipped the other vehicle over. This ill-fated car had five people inside of it. All were injured and some would not make it through the ordeal. Busby in the meantime, had a couple of passengers with him— one of them unconscious. He and his buddy William Hudson struggled to pull the unconscious man out.

It was shortly after they were all free from the wreckage, that Busby's car actually ignited. Busby at this point, apparently had a complete nervous breakdown. Leaving his passengers and the victims of the other car behind, he simply walked away. In a numb and confused state, he walked all the way to a local coffee shop, where he went inside begging for someone, *anyone* to give him a ride.

Busby kept muttering, "I have to get away. They will be looking for me soon." Although Busby never said "the police will be looking for me" it was quite clear to those who heard him, that this was precisely what he was referring to. Such things would be pretty damning at Busby's trial since they seemed to indicate that he was knowingly trying to flee the scene of an accident.

But Busby couldn't escape; the police actually tracked him down to the coffee shop and began questioning him right then and there. Busby was entirely evasive in his answers and actually tried to say that he wasn't driving at the time of the crash. It was only when he realized that this wouldn't fly that he grudgingly admitted that he was indeed the driver, and therefore he was the one responsible for the terrible accident that had just occurred.

As much as he was grudgingly accepting responsibility at this point—his next few remarks, seemed to negate them. When he was asked why he was trying to "leave the scene of the accident" he answered that he was simply wanting to "call his mother." Busby had left people bleeding and dying, just to chat with his mom. The responding officers who heard all of this must have taken it in with a mixture of humor, horror, and disgust.

The Suspect

Busby Berkeley could not escape taking some sort of responsibility for his actions, and was subsequently put on trial for "second-degree murder." Interestingly enough, even though he had walked away from the accident just fine, by the time his case went to trial, he was making appearances being wheeled into the courtroom on a stretcher.

This approach was no doubt fully sanctioned by his attorney Jerry Giesler, who had made a career of defending the indefensible. It was no doubt advised that Busby milk any of his own possible injuries for what they were worth—in order to elicit as much sympathy as possible. Whatever the case may be, the plan seemed to work. Busby ended up facing two hung juries, before being acquitted the third time around.

The third time was indeed the charm, and Busby Berkeley made quite a show of his own acquittal, even posing for pictures for the Associated Press. For this photo op, he was impeccably dressed, in a nice suit complete with a matching handkerchief. Even his dear old mother was there with him, wearing her best brooch and hat.

Busby Berkeley had the following to say for himself at the time: "I was lucky that I had so much work because it helped keep my mind off the accident. Even though I was found innocent, it was a shocking and terribly depressing thing to have been involved in the death of three people."

In the End

Depressing indeed. *So* depressing in fact, that Berkley would be haunted by this event for the rest of his life. And in 1946, he would attempt to commit suicide. He would recover and would ultimately die of natural causes at the ripe old age of 80, but he never really was quite the same after that. It took much of his fortune just to pay his legal fees, as well as a $95,000 settlement.

So, what is the final verdict as it pertains to public opinion? Is Busby Berkeley a murderer? Or was his tragic accident just that—a tragic accident? The jury may still be out as it pertains to public opinion, and as it pertains to this supposed spate of Hollywood Homicides—we'll just have to let the reader decide for themself.

Was Brittany Murphy Murdered?

Who*:* Brittany Murphy
Where: Hollywood, California
When: December 2009
Suspects*:* Simon Monjack
Conviction*:* None

Background Information

She was a rising star who starred in films such as "Drop Dead Gorgeous" and "Girl, Interrupted." Both of these films would cement her as an up-and-coming talent. But ultimately, Brittany Murphy was perhaps best known for her role in the Eminem biopic "Eight Mile" in which she played the rapper's then-girlfriend.

Baby Brittany made her debut in the world in Atlanta, Georgia, in the year 1977. Her life was troubled from the beginning, due to the instability of her parents. Her father was a habitual offender who was frequently serving stints in prison, and Brittany was largely raised by her mother, Sharon. Despite these hard times, however, Brittany was encouraged by her mother to pursue the fine arts. She took dancing and acting classes, starting at the tender age of 5.

These lessons paid off, and by the time she was a young teenager, she was being given a walk on parts for television sitcoms such as "Boy Meets World," "Sister, Sister," and even "Murphy Brown." Her real breakout role, however, came when she was tapped to play the part of "Alicia Silverstone" in the 1995 hit—"Clueless." It was after this breakthrough, that she would end up appearing in major motion pictures such as "Girl Interrupted," "8 Mile," and "Sin City."

She was flying high, but her spirits seemed to dampen a bit when she hooked up with Simon Monjack. Mr. Monjack was seven years older than Brittany, yet had a career that seemed to be floundering, even as Brittany's was on the ascent. Monjack was a screenwriter who hailed from Britain. Monjack had seen better days, however, and by the time he and Brittany were an item, he was having a terribly hard time finding work for his craft.

Friends and family were surprised by the sudden whirlwind romance that led to Murphy marrying Monjack. The actress seemed to have everything going for her, and her pick of any eligible bachelor, and yet she settled for this man, for whom her peers did not see much of a future.

But as they say, love is in the eyes of the beholder, and even though others may not have understood her attraction to Simon Monjack—Brittany Murphy clearly was in love with the man.

It was immediately after her marriage to Monjack however, that Brittany's mood seemed to dramatically change. In the past she was known to be quite easy to work with; but after marrying Monjack, she was found to be difficult on the set. She also appeared to be rapidly losing weight. She was already thin, yet now she was becoming downright skeletal. Perhaps not surprisingly, Brittany's friends blamed all of these things on Simon Monjack.

On That Day

In December of 2009, Brittany's promising career would come to a sudden end when the then 32-year-old actress was found unconscious and unresponsive in her LA home. She was rushed to Cedars-Sinai Medical Center, where she died and was unable to be revived. Initially, her cause of death would be ruled as pneumonia. The ruling was a rather curious one, and several drugs would be subsequently found in her system, upon being given an autopsy.

The ruling would then switch to that of an accidental overdose, just before she was laid to rest, at Forest Lawn Hollywood Hills cemetery on December 24th, 2009. This was not the end of this strange story, however, because her husband Simon Monjack, would be found dead roughly a year later, at the same house, under very similar conditions.

The Suspect(s)

Even before Brittany Murphy died, Simon Monjack had been held under suspicion, of being a negative influence on her life. Her death of course only exacerbated these suspicions. Hollywood reporter Amber Ryland famously interviewed Monjack in the aftermath of Brittany's demise, and she too would later recall that she couldn't help but wonder if she was interviewing "a murderer."

After Brittany passed, even those who did not directly suggest that Monjack was a murderer, intimated that he had somehow contributed to her death by "allowing her" to get so thin. Such claims, however, are a bit absurd when we consider the fact that Brittany was a 32-year-old adult. As much as folks want to point the finger at Monjack, at the end of the day, it was up to Brittany to keep herself healthy.

Nevertheless, the suspicions would continue. Especially in the immediate aftermath of Brittany's death, when reporter Amber Ryland paid Monjack a visit, and came back with startling reports of the widower's lifestyle. Most alarming according to this witness, was Monjack's relationship with Brittany's mother, Sharon.

Simon Monjack was apparently allowing Brittany's mother to stay with him, even after Brittany's death. Now, someone with a more generous view would probably applaud this man for being kind enough to open his home up to his former mother-in-law.

But those with deep suspicions in their minds might perceive this good deed, as something more sinister—*even creepy*. And Ryland, after seeing an unmade bed at the home, actually went so far as to insinuate that the two slept together. Without even coming right out and saying it, the suggestion is clear—Monjack was being accused of having romantic relations with his dead wife's mom.

But even though such wild insinuations have been made, there has never been any clear evidence that this was ever the case. Nevertheless, a lack of clear-cut facts did not stop the rumor mills of suspicion. Not at all helping his cause, was the fact that Monjack himself tried to thwart an autopsy of his wife. Such things do indeed raise some red flags—but even so, his mere attempt to prevent an autopsy is not a smoking gun indication that this guy is a killer.

It could just be that he wanted privacy, or simply did not want the nude body of his wife poked around and messed with by the coroner. It's easy to point fingers and blame others without understanding the point of view of those who are having to make some very difficult decisions.

Nevertheless, even after Simon Monjack himself perished, there were those that continued to point their fingers at him, even as he was being lowered into the grave. For them, Monjack's death itself was nothing more than a sign of his own guilt, since it was suggested that perhaps he had committed suicide because he was unable to live with what he had done to Brittany. Out of all of this, however, the only thing that could be said for certain is that Brittany's friends *did not like Monjack.*

In the End

But just because they hated this guy's guts, does not mean that he was the killer. It just means that they despised this person and held him in deep suspicion. Despite all of their suspicions, however, there is no proof that he killed Brittany Murphy. But if it wasn't Simon Monjack—then just who or what was it, that actually led to her final demise? Many questions remain.

Carl Switzer
That Little Rascal, Alfalfa

Who*:* Carl Switzer
Where: Mission Hill, California
When: January 21, 1959
Suspects*:* Moses Stiltz
Conviction*:* None

Background Information

Although the world knew him as "Alfalfa" his name at birth was Carl Switzer. Carl was born in Paris, Illinois, on the 7th of August, in the year 1927. He was the son of one George and Gladys Switzer. The youngest of four children, this future Alfalfa was the final installment in a rambunctious and restless family.

Carl and his brother Harold would grow up as natural clowns, who were always getting into all manner of hijinks. It was from these early family experiences that the hyperactive Alfalfa character would arise.

The boys not only played practical jokes but also developed singing and musical ability, learning several musical instruments at a time. The boys' parents must have realized that their kids had talent, and they were foresighted enough to encourage their gifts. This desire to encourage the boys would then turn into an unexpected necessity when the original breadwinner of the family—George Switzer—lost a foot in a terrible accident at his workplace.

With George unable to work due to his injury, it actually becomes incumbent upon Carl and Harold to attempt to make enough cash through their performances to help the family scrape by. The boys would often take part in local fairs in Illinois, and any other open-ended venue in which they could pass around a hat and have some money tossed in it. This was initially just a part-time gig to help the family, but a major turning point would come when Carl and Harold were brought out to California to see some long-lost relatives.

During the course of the trip, the boys begged their mom and dad to take them over to Hal Roach Studio. Mr. and Mrs. Switzer didn't know what the big deal was, but they readily obliged. The reason the boys were so interested in the studio was due to the fact that this was the place where a popular series of film skits called "Our Gang" was being developed.

The series of shorts depicted a hyper bunch of kids engaged in all manner of comical hijinks. In other words—it was right up Carl and Harold's alley. They wanted to star in the show for themselves. It was with this in mind that Carl and his brother were shown around Hal Roach studios. Initially, they were just fans passing through, but their golden opportunity came when they sat down at the cafeteria for a bite to eat.

It was here that the then 6-year-old Carl Switzer and his 8-year-old brother Harold did something bold. They hopped up onto a table and began randomly dancing and singing. For any other kids their age, this would have been a sure source of embarrassment for all of the adults in the room—but these youngsters didn't embarrass anyone. On the contrary, they gained the eyes and ears of promoters, who immediately saw potential in the antics of these two kids.

In fact, they managed to impress none other than Hal Roach, who just so happened to be in the room when the spontaneous act exploded. It was Mr. Roach who then walked right up to the boys' mother and father and suggested that they perform some skits for the "Our Gang" series. That's all that Roach had to say, and soon enough, Carl and Harold both had their names put in a contract. The two brothers would then make their debut in 1935 on an "Our Gang" piece called "Beginners Luck."

It was in this piece that Carl would first appear as "Alfalfa," whereas his bother Harold would be called "Slim." From the beginning, however, it was Carl's Alfalfa who stole the show. For who could forget the freckled kid with the mile-long cowlick of hair sticking up on the back of his head? After three shorts were produced with the young brothers, Carl emerged as the clear favorite, and Alfalfa became the starring role, whereas Harold's Slim was made into an increasingly minor one.

With a solid line up formulated, "Our Gang" would transform into "The Little Rascals" in 1938. And over the next couple of years, Carl Switzer would be a leading star of the production. It seems that during this period, Switzer knowing his importance, became a bit arrogant. It's said that he would often throw "tantrums" off camera and he would play all kinds of practical jokes on hapless crew members.

The jokes were funny when written into the script, but these off-script antics caused some real-life duress. As was the case when Carl decided to literally gum up the works by putting chewing gum in the gears of the cameraman's camera. Or even worse, the time he urinated on top of set lights, causing them to fizzle and fail; leaving a bad ammonia smell as the set went into darkness.

As bad as his antics were, they were largely overlooked because of the perceived comedic value that this wild child brought to "The Little Rascals". Carl Switzer had a little problem, however—he was growing up fast. By 1940, he was 13 and rapidly entering adolescence. Switzer found himself face to face with the problem of many child stars: he had simply outgrown his role. He wasn't the cute kid anymore, and soon "The Little Rascals" had no more room for him.

Switzer left the production behind and tried to expand his reach into new roles. Initially, it went well enough. Switzer had already developed the tenuous Hollywood connections that many other artists spend years struggling to get. He was able to get booked for several films. Switzer even managed to appear in the Christmas classic "It's a Wonderful Life." His role is often overlooked, but Switzer played the part of one "Freddie Othelo."

Freddie was the future Mary Bailey character's teenage date for the prom. He was the guy who talked Mary's ear off before the George Bailey character walked up and told him to "go annoy someone else." By the early 1950s however, Switzer's acting roles began to dry up, and unable to get booked for the Silver Screen, he only managed to secure a few minor parts on TV.

One of his most frequent gigs was a recurring role on the Roy Rogers Show, where he appeared on six different occasions. It was actually while gigging for Roy Rogers, that Carl would meet the man who would later kill him—Samuel 'Bud' Stiltz.

In the meantime, Switzer would get married in 1954 to Diantha Collingwood, who was an "heiress" to the massive Collingwood Grain company which was quite lucrative at the time. The couple had a son—Justin—shortly after they got hitched, and of course, this new addition made it even more incumbent upon Carl to get his act together (both literally and figuratively).

Carl proved entirely unstable however, and his wife fed up with a man who didn't seem to have a future, kicked him to the curb in 1957. It was after his marriage fell apart that Carl would return to

California, and play bit parts in TV shows. In between these minor gigs, he worked as a bartender and also took up a job arranging hunting tours.

Carl had long been an avid hunter, and along with acting, it was one of the few things he enjoyed in life. The other thing he enjoyed was drinking—and drinking quite heavily. After a night of several rounds of drinks in 1958, Switzer left a bar only to be ambushed. He got into his car when someone rolled up and shot him. He was hit in his right arm, and was bleeding profusely—but he would live.

Police, however, were entirely unable to determine who his assailant was. The incident would remain a mystery, and as terrible as it was, Carl Switzer would soon put it to the back of his mind. For he had more pressing concerns—such as making enough money to keep a roof over his head. Always short of money, Switzer began to delve into practices that were not exactly on the up and up.

It was during the Christmas season of 1958 that he would get in trouble over a scheme he had concocted to make a little money. He was spotted up in Sequoia National Forest illegally cutting down several stately pine trees he hoped to sell for those desiring authentic Christmas trees. For this offense, he was put on probation and ordered to pay out $225 in damages. Switzer closed out the year 1958 with plenty of problems—but it would be January of 1959 that would really do him in.

On That Day

It was in January of 1959, that Carl Switzer got himself into a real sticky situation. He had been hanging out with his old buddy Moses Stiltz when Moses gave him permission to use one of his hunting dogs for a bear hunt that Switzer was leading. Switzer took part in these forays for extra cash, and unlike his tree-cutting adventures, this was perfectly legal. Switzer's outing would come to grief however when the prized hunting dog ran off and wouldn't come back.

Switzer knew that he would be in trouble with Moses for losing the dog, so he immediately put up an ad and even posted a reward for the return of the animal. He lucked out when a short time later a guy actually showed up at Switzer's workplace with the dog. Switzer gave him the $35 reward as well as several drinks on the house. Carl Switzer then returned the dog to Moses Stiltz and everything seemed to have been squared away.

It was then on January 21st, that a strange idea entered Carl Switzer's head. He had been drinking heavily with some buddies when he suddenly decided to get the reward money back from Moses Stiltz. For some reason, Switzer had convinced himself that he was entitled to the reward money he himself had posted for the return of the dog he had lost. Such logic makes no sense to a sober mind, but in Carl Switzer's inebriated state, it seemed to be somehow almost logical.

After Switzer barged into Stiltz's home demanding the cash, Moses Stiltz of course was none too pleased. An argument ensued, and at some point, it got physical. Although the accounts have varied through the years, it seems that Stiltz was struck in the head by Switzer with a glass clock of some sort. Stiltz then took off to a back room, before returning with a gun. The two men then fought over the weapon, and according to Stiltz it "accidentally" went off, hitting Switzer in the belly.

The Suspect

Moses Stiltz always denied killing Carl Switzer. Others, however, would suggest that perhaps it wasn't an accident and that Switzer was intentionally murdered. In January of 2001 in fact, many years after Stiltz himself had already passed—his stepson Tom Corrigan, came forward to suggest that Carl Switzer was indeed the victim of a homicide.

According to Corrigan, who was there that night, Switzer, when confronted with the firearm, had turned to leave. Tom Corrigan apparently thought that this was the end of the confrontation, but the next thing he knew a shot was fired. Corrigan didn't see the shot, he only heard it—but immediately after the shot rang out, he looked over to see Switzer fall down dead. Corrigan is certain that Switzer was shot even after he was trying to disengage and leave the scene.

In the End

It's for this reason that Tom Corrigan is of the belief that the killing was not self-defense, as Moses Stiltz had claimed, but pure and simple homicide. Yes, even many years after the fact, the exact details of Carl Switzer's death are still very hard to fathom.

Sal Mineo—Misunderstood in Both Life and Death

Who*:* Sal Mineo
Where: Hollywood, California
When: February 1976
Suspects*:* Lionel Williams
Conviction*:* March 1979

Background Information

Sal Mineo was the son of an immigrant. His father Salvatore made his way to the United States of America from the Italian island of Sicily in 1929. Salvatore was just 16 years of age when he arrived on American shores, but despite his relative youth and inexperience, he was ready to make something of himself. He worked hard, serving as a carpenter and bricklayer for various odd jobs.

He was also a bit of an entrepreneur, demonstrated by the fact that he would whittle small little statues out of left-over wood from the job, and then sell them for profit. Salvatore would soon meet the love of his life in America, one Josephine Alvisi. The couple would ultimately get married when they were both 18 years of age, in 1931.

It was from this union that Sal (or Salvatore Junior) was born on January 10th, 1939. At the time of Sal's birth, his dad was employed in a rather grim environment, at Bronx Casket Company, toiling away as a casket maker. The Salvatore senior did a good job but felt he wasn't getting paid enough, so in 1946 he embarked upon establishing his own business, Universal Casket Company.

The name might have been a bit generic—but it worked. The company began in the family basement, where Salvatore labored for hours on end, crafting the finest wooden caskets possible. Salvatore's wife helped out by essentially becoming the bookkeeper of the company setting up appointments and keeping the finances straight. It was a true labor of love, but to make it work the couple had to put in long hours.

This often left their four children to their own devices. Sal, in fact, was often his little sister's live-in baby-sitter. Sal didn't mind his living situation so much, but he would often get picked on by other kids, who thought it was spooky that his dad worked on caskets. Neighborhood taunts led to Sal learning to become tough, so he could better fend off the bullies.

Sal Mineo grew up in Catholic schools, and it was at a Catholic school that he first learned to act. He was tapped for a school production to play the role of Jesus. There's certainly no bigger role than that—and Sal loved the attention he received for his efforts. The casket business was picking up in the meantime, and the family was able to move to a larger home in a more prosperous section of the Bronx.

Their new residence had enough rooms for everyone and even an office for Josephine to work in as she continued to do bookkeeping for the family business. Sal was having problems at school, however, and these Bronx bullies proved to be particularly aggressive. At one point, in fact, one of them actually pulled a knife on Sal. Sal, however, impressed his peers when he singlehandedly disarmed his assailant.

Sal had made it quite clear that he could stick up for himself, and from this point forward, he was no longer targeted by the would-be tough guys at his school. Sal was someone whom others took notice of, as was demonstrated one fine day in 1948 when young Sal was approached by an agent right in the middle of the street. The agent said that Sal had potential, and with a little direction, he could probably become an actor on television.

Young Sal took the man to meet his mother, but she didn't take the stranger quite so seriously. Even so, after getting the guy's business card, she took him up on the suggestion that Sal should get dancing lessons to refine some of his budding talents. The lessons weren't cheap, however, and Sal ended up working a part-time job as a newspaper boy, in order to help pay for them. The lessons would pay off, however, when Sal was recruited to dance for "The Ted Steele Show."

Even so, it was still all Sal's parents could do at times just to keep Sal out of trouble. When he wasn't dancing, he was running with a tough crowd and was often having brushes with the law for petty crimes such as vandalism and theft. It was in a bid to keep Sal out of trouble that his parents sought to continue to nourish his artistic streak and sent Sal off to acting school.

Shortly thereafter, Sal attracted the attention of a talent scout. One thing led to another, and the next thing anyone knew Sal was making his debut on Broadway. The part he was cast for was not a big one, and he had only one line in the hall play—but the fact that he was even on stage was a great boon to Sal's confidence. Sal was soon regularly taking the stage, and would get his big break when he was recruited to take part in a Tennessee Williams play called "The Rose Tattoo."

His success prompted his parents to pull him out of the school he hated, and he would finish up the rest of his primary education by way of a tutor. His next major gig would then come when he was cast for the role of "Crown Prince of Siam, Chulalongkorn" in the epic play "The King and I."

Sal did well enough but would embarrass himself royally before it was all said and done. One night as he was bowing at the end of the play, his belt somehow came loose and he accidentally dropped his drawers right in front of the audience. Audience members may have thought this was a planned comedic routine, but it was no joke, and Sal of course was mortified. Nevertheless, the play had a good run, and by the time of its closing in 1954, Sal had performed as Chulalongkorn hundreds of times.

This success was followed up by another when Sal was recruited to take part in the move "Rebel without a Cause." Sal was tapped to reprise the role of the Dean character's side-kick "Plato." Initially, Mineo had a hard time getting to know the dashing Dean. After a while, however, the two managed to break the ice and got along with each other quite well.

This chemistry came through to film goers, and the movie itself, of course, was a box office hit. For his work in the picture, Sal would end up getting a nomination for "Best Supporting Actor." All of these accolades paved the way for Sal to be chosen to play the character "Jack Lemmon" in the film "Mr. Roberts."

Shortly after this film, Sal would go on to star in a war flick called "Giant." Dean was also in this picture, and it would be his last since the heartthrob actor would perish shortly after it was produced. Sal would continue his work, however, and in 1956 would star with actor Paul Newman in the film "Somebody Up There Likes Me." It was on the heels of this movie, that Sal would be cast as "Angelo" in the movie "Crime in the Streets."

This film would catapult Sal right into the American consciousness, with his catchy one-liners striking a chord with movie goers. Even while he was making it big in the movies, Sal sought to try out another avenue—*music.* For it was around this time that he actually recorded the song "Start Movin'". The song managed to hit the Top Ten, but his musical talent was ultimately not as appealing as his acting talent, and by 1959, Sal decided to put all of his focus on the movie business.

Even so, his next role as the actor had him portraying musical genius Gene Krupa, in "The Gene Krupa Story." It was immediately following this film, however, that Sal would truly gain widescale recognition when he starred in the film "Exodus" as a holocaust survivor. He played the part of Don Landau, a kid who had managed to survive the horrors of the holocaust, even though he had lost his whole family in the process. It was a comprehensive and serious role that won him much acclaim. Sal figured he was a shoo-in for an Oscar.

Sal, however, was ultimately disappointed when he ended up losing his bid for the award to Peter Ustinov who had just appeared in the epic film "Spartacus." Despite his own growing success, Sal was beginning to take things personally in the movie business and was sensitive to any perceived slights. This bitterness seemed to all but consume Sal Mineo, it affected his future work and the parts he took became smaller and smaller.

He managed to rebound a bit in 1965 however when he appeared in the movie "Who Killed Teddybear?" But after this film, his roles became increasingly obscure. By the 1970s, Sal was still working, but only enough to get by. It was only in 1976, that Sal managed to score a larger role when he was hired to act in a comedy thriller called "PS Your Cat is Dead." This film promised to give Sal a larger, more multifaceted role.

On That Day

It was during the production of his latest film, on February 12th, 1976, that Sal himself would die. It was late that evening, that some of Sal's neighbors suddenly heard the sound of him screaming outside of the apartment in which he lived. They ran out, and found Sal on the ground in the fetal position, with blood pouring out of him. Emergency services were called, but the then 37-year-old Sal Mineo perished from his wounds before they could arrive.

The Investigation

The subsequent investigation into Mineo's death would end up ensnaring a man by the name of Lionel Williams. Mr. Williams was initially accused of the crime by his own wife, who was familiar with the circumstances of Mineo's death and had seen her husband arrive at their home "covered in blood" on the evening that Mineo had perished.

Lionel had already been picked up for bad check charges in the meantime, and several inmates claimed that they had overheard him actually openly boasting of killing the actor. There was some confusion and doubt over whether Lionel was the killer or not, however, during the subsequent trial, the killer had been described by later witnesses, as a guy with "long brown hair." Lionel Williams on the other hand, didn't seem to fit this description, since he was an African American man with dark, shorter hair.

The notion that it was indeed Lionel Williams however, was bolstered when prosecutors revealed a photo of Williams with "straightened" long hair, that had been dyed brown. Despite any later alterations, in this particular picture, Williams did indeed have long brown hair, just as the witnesses had described. Nevertheless, Lionel Williams' own sister would come forward with a different story as to who the killer might be. She claimed that Sal was killed over drugs, and her brother was actually taking the fall for a buddy of his.

In the End

There was never any proof of any of this, however, and in the Spring of 1979, Lionel Williams was indeed convicted of Sal Mineo's murder and received 51 years to life for the killing. But there are those to this day who still question this verdict, and many still wonder how Sal Mineo met his end. This is quite sad since Sal himself often felt so misunderstood in life. So it is, in full sad irony to say, that as much as Sal was misunderstood in life, he was also misunderstood in death.

Christa Helm
Stardom Interrupted

Who: Christa Helm
Where: New York, New York
When: February 1977
Suspects: Unknown
Conviction: None

Background Information

Christa Helm had a troubled and abbreviated life. She sought
stardom in Hollywood, but really never rose to the occasion.
Other than being a hanger-on of celebrities—she never really
became one herself. Her only real claim to fame was the fact that
she died under some very shady and mysterious circumstances.
Nevertheless, she began life with much promise, when she was
born in November of 1949.

She was the oldest of three daughters, born to Harry and
Dolores Wohlfeil. But sadly enough, Christa's parents would go
their separate ways when Christa was still just a child. Her father
would then go on to marry another woman and start a family with
her—seemingly leaving his old family behind. Christa's mother in
the meantime, would end up seeing a whole string of boyfriends,
many of them quite abusive to their mother and the girls too.

Things were so bad, that her previously absentee father decided
to step in, and had his daughters come live with him and his
newly established family. Still, Christa was troubled and had
problems. She had to wear a back brace due to spinal issues
and was looking for emotional support. As she entered her teens
and grew into an attractive young woman, she sought that
emotional support in male companionship. This would lead a 16-
year-old Christa Helm, to enter into a relationship with one "Gary
Clements" who was in his mid-20s at the time of the relationship.

It's said that Gary got his young girlfriend pregnant fairly soon
into their relationship. They got married in Chicago, but as soon

as baby Nicole was born, Gary split and was never seen again. There was even some speculation that perhaps he was killed—but ultimately neither Christa nor anyone else seemed to know what had happened to the guy. Christa in the meantime, managed to get a job waiting tables at an Italian bistro in Milwaukee. It wasn't much, but it paid some bills.

It was while she worked as a waitress, that she became friends with a co-worker—Diane Mitchell. Ms. Mitchell was a few years older than Christa, but immediately aware that the teenager was wise beyond her years, Mitchell was drawn in by her outgoing personality. The two also had something in common, since they were both single mothers.

They were not always the most responsible of single mothers, however, since ultimately the pair opted to move into an apartment together, while sloughing off the full-time duties of parenting on their own moms, rather than taking full-time care of their kids themselves. Yes, both Christa's daughter Nicole as well as Ms. Mitchell's daughter Kellena, were practically raised by their grandmothers, while only seeing their high-rolling moms on the weekends if they were lucky.

Christa, free from the responsibility of parenting for much of the rest of her time, regularly self-indulged in a seemingly carefree life of partying. Mitchell became a little concerned, however, when it seemed that Christa Helm sometimes had a complete lack of discretion as it pertained to who she partied with. Her friend told her to be careful who she invited over, but Christa Helm would simply insist that her roommate "worried too much."

Mitchell would later recall that Christa drank and also smoked marijuana—but didn't recall her engaging in any hard drugs. Christa Helm's desire to become *somebody* in Hollywood came about, after she and her roommate Mitchell, found themselves in attendance at a party thrown at the Playboy Club in Lake Geneva, Wisconsin. Here they were able to meet a star performer—James Darren—backstage. It was in the rush of all of this excitement, that the two vivacious young women determined that they would like to become "Playboy bunnies."

They put in an application and were hired. After receiving their proper "bunny fittings" they then began work. They were also given lodgings in a dorm, where they received special training on how to serve food and drinks for the establishment. Mitchell's mother became the spoiler in all of their fun, however, by suddenly insisting that Ms. Mitchell take care of her daughter, rather than train her to be a playboy bunny!

Most of us upon hearing all of this, would probably agree with Mitchell's mother on this one, that her priorities were pretty out of whack. Nevertheless, Mitchell was frustrated that her mother had tossed "a monkey wrench" into all of her plans. It was this bit of leverage used by Mitchell's mom anyway, that ended up having both Christa Helm and Diane Mitchell calling the whole thing off.

Christa and Diane would find someone else to pawn their children off on, however; one "Mrs. Gertrude Baker" who was the mother of a mutual friend. They apparently dropped their daughters off into the care of Gertrude and then went on to try their luck modeling in New York City. With not much more than their own ambition to get them through, the two young women got themselves a place to stay at the YWCA and looked through the want ads every chance they could.

The reception they received was not what they wanted, however, with Mitchell later admitting that many of the want ads were "seedy" people seeking only to exploit young women in the vilest way, rather than any legitimate modeling work. The two eventually got jobs as waitresses and managed to hold things down on their own, but Diane Mitchell grew weary of the grind and decided to leave New York and head back to Milwaukee.

Christa in the meantime, was hob-knobbing with the stars whenever she could and eventually ended up becoming the girlfriend of an NFL player—Ray Abbruzzese. Ray was a long-time great who had played for both the Buffalo Bills as well as the New York Jets. As much of a cliché as it might have been, just being seen arm and arm with Abbruzzese was enough to raise Christa's profile significantly.

Christa began taking acting and singing lessons in the meantime, attempting to better hone her craft. Mitchell kept in touch and would learn that in Christa's incredibly fast-paced life, by 1971, she had already forgotten all about her old flame Ray

Abbruzzese, and instead had begun to see a rich Broadway director by the name of Stuart Duncan.

Duncan was also a direct heir to the Lee & Perrin Worcestershire Sauce company. It might be funny to think of someone being linked to all of that tasty Worcestershire Sauce, but his connection to this lucrative company's big bucks was no joke and meant that Stuart Duncan was pretty much rolling in money. Duncan, therefore, seemed to check off many of the boxes that Christa desired, he was rich and famous; as well as entirely well connected to the arts, from his perch on Broadway.

It was no doubt with these new connections that Christa Helm began to improve her own career prospects. Soon, she was getting booked for lucrative modeling gigs all over New York. She was now out of the YWCA and had moved into an extravagant apartment all on her own. Christa Helm got herself a flashy new Corvette, while she was at it—and began to run with a crowd of rich and famous folks up in the exclusive New York neighborhood of the Hamptons.

It was around this time that Diane Mitchell paid Christa Helm a visit, and noted her apparent success in the modeling business. She also noted the fact that Christa had some plastic surgery work done. To Diane Mitchell's surprise, Christa Helm had gone under the knife to make her breasts bigger.

At any rate, Diane thought Christa seemed happy and excited about the direction her life was taking. But she also noted a bit of cynicism that had seemed to take root inside the psyche of her old friend. Christa Helm, it seemed, had witnessed the dark side of the high life. She had seen how folks routinely rise and fall. Christa now knew that in this cutthroat business, even the highest of penthouse rooftops was only a few steps removed from the gutter.

At this point, she had become acquainted with one Jeremiah Newton who was a regular at the famed Stonewall Inn in Greenwich Village. It was around this time that Christa Helm made her film debut, by playing a part in the 1972 horror movie called "The Legacy of Satan." Duncan in the meantime had transitioned from Broadway to producing films, and recruited

Helm to work on his new piece "Let's Go For Broke." In this film, Christa was given the role of a reporter named "Jackie Broke."

After filming, Helm returned to New York and continued to live it up, dating several well-known men including NFL star Joe Namath, and producer Joseph Middleton. At one point, she even dated Mick Jagger from the Rolling Stones. Even so, she was still struggling to break into the big time. Her most well-known contributions to date, in fact, were nothing better than a walk-on role as a "roller skating waitress" in the TV show "Starsky and Hutch" and as a random beauty contestant in "Wonder Woman."

In the meantime, she was still waiting for her contributions in "Let's Go For Broke" to get noticed. But the film didn't seem to be going anywhere. Christa ended up switching gears and began pursuing work as a singer. It was now the late 1970s, and Helm wished to make a "disco" album. She began working with a couple of female backup singers during the process and became intimately involved with one of them—Patty Collins.

On That Day

It was in the midst of this project, that Christa would meet her end, when on February 12th, of 1977, after a night of unabashed partying, she turned up dead. She was brutally assaulted after leaving the party and walking to her car. She is said to have been stabbed numerous times and beaten in the head. The assault apparently happened very quickly, and whoever the assailant was then fled the scene.

A passerby, in fact, came across Christa shortly after the event transpired. He walked up to find her on the ground. The witness apparently heard her breathe out one last ragged breath, right before she expired.

In the End

This terrible murder is still unsolved but has haunted investigators for decades. Whoever the assailant was, it seemed that they were determined to kill this woman no matter what.

Christa's death does not seem to be the result of simply an aggressive robber or any other sort of random assailant.

The pure ferocity of the attack, makes it seem more like a purposeful hit, carried out by someone determined to snuff out Christa Helm's young life. Did she make some powerful enemies somewhere along the way? Perhaps. As it pertains to this homicide—there's still much that we simply don't know.

Haing S. Ngor and the Killing Fields of the Khmer Rouge

Who*:* Haing S. Ngor
Where: Los Angeles, California
When: February 1996
Suspects*:* Gang hit - Pol Pot
Conviction*:* April 1998

Background Information

Dr. Haing S. Ngor was a survivor. He had survived the literal "killing fields" of Cambodia and made his way to the United States as a young man. Prior to fleeing his home country, he began a career as a physician and had a young wife, who had died in childbirth, no thanks to the ruthless regime of the Khmer Rouge.

He had survived these only to make his way to the United States, where he was later gunned down in his home by some two-bit hoodlums, simply because he would not hand over a gold locket that held a photo of his beloved former wife.

In between all of this, Dr. Ngor had become quite famous, due to his starring in a story about the tragedies that had unfolded in Cambodia, by way of the 1984 film, "The Killing Fields." His role as the refugee "Pran" in this moving piece, managed to garner Dr. Ngor an Oscar. All of this would come to an end, however, when Dr. Ngor was murdered in 1996, at the age of just 55 years old.

Born in 1940, Dr. Ngor began life in the Cambodian village of Samrong Young, which at that time was under the occupation of the French. Ngor was just a small child when the French were overwhelmed by a Japanese invasion. Much of what was then known as French Indochina which consisted of Cambodia, Laos, and Vietnam, then came under the control of the Japanese.

After Japan was defeated in 1945, at the close of World War Two, the French attempted to reassert themselves but were confronted by many insurgent groups; most notably the communists in North Vietnam. The French were ultimately defeated in 1954, and the U.S. would take up the struggle against the North Vietnamese. Cambodia in the meantime would gain independence.

Initially, Cambodia was an independent, U.S.-friendly nation, known as the "Khmer Republic" which attempted to maintain neutrality during the conflict in Vietnam. After U.S. forces were defeated, and Vietnam fell to communism, however, a brutal regime known as the "Khmer Rouge" led by a savage dictator by the name of Pol Pot took over and initiated a reign of terror in Cambodia that lasted from 1975 to 1979.

Ngor had just begun work as a doctor when the Khmer Rouge took over. Since the communist-backed Khmer Rouge despised anyone perceived to be of the intelligentsia, or upwardly mobile, Ngor felt the need to conceal his practice as a physician.

He closed up shop and even stopped wearing glasses. That was just how oppressive the Khmer Rouge was. Just imagine standing on the street corner minding your own business, wearing a pair of prescription eye glasses, when a thug from the Khmer Rouge confronts you.

The Khmer Rouge tough guy pokes you in the chest and shouts, "Oh! You wear glasses! You must read a lot of books! You must think you're real smart, huh?" As ridiculous as it sounds, these were indeed the sort of things going on in Cambodia. And it was for this reason, that Dr. Ngor feared wearing his glasses in public.

But no matter how careful Dr. Ngor was to avoid both the scrutiny and the wrath of the Khmer Rouge, during their so-called "Year Zero" socialist experiment, in which they tried to recreate society in their own image, Dr. Ngor was inevitably rounded up and detained.

He and his spouse My-Huoy were shuffled off to what was essentially a concentration camp. My-Huoy was pregnant and expecting her baby at any time. Despite her condition, proper medical care and even basic comforts were denied her. My-Huoy faced complications during the delivery and both she and the baby died right then and there at the concentration camp.

Adding to all of the bitter ironies, Dr. Ngor as a doctor, knew how to save his wife. He knew that she needed a Caesarian section, and he knew how to carry one out. Yet, even he was not permitted to use his own skilled hands as a surgeon, to aid his dying wife, since the Khmer Rouge on the hunt for intellectuals, would have simply killed the doctor as soon as they learned of his true profession.

Yes, in this bizarre backdrop of socialist experimentation, many suffered and many died—Ngor's wife and child ultimately being among them. Dr. Ngor himself would escape, however, making his way to the United States as a refugee, in the year 1980. It was after he resettled in America that he wrote a book about his experiences, entitled, *Haing Ngor: A Cambodian Odyssey.*

This book would later be revised as *The Killing Fields.* The movie of the same name would be released in 1984, and Haing, even though he had no prior training in the field, worked as a supporting actor, playing himself on the silver screen. The movie was a great success at the box office, and Haing would actually go on to win Oscar, in the category of "Best Supporting Actor."

After achieving this feat, Dr. Ngo's words appeared in *People Magazine,* where he went on the record to state, "I wanted to show the world how deep starvation is in Cambodia, how many people die under the communist regime. My heart is satisfied." Dr. Ngo was satisfied that his portrayal in the film had revealed to a wider audience the terrors of the Khmer Rouge in particular and communist totalitarian regimes in general. He felt that his life's work had been achieved.

It is somewhat heartening to know that he was at least fulfilled in this manner, since his life would be cut so tragically short. Not long after he uttered these encouraging, thought-provoking words. Interestingly enough, "The Killing Fields" was not the only Hollywood production in which Dr. Ngo appeared. Ngo also starred in the Oliver Stone flick called "Heaven & Earth," in 1993, and also appeared in a miniseries called "Vanishing Son."

Also in 1993, he starred in a production of the movie "My Life." This was perhaps his most memorable role. In this film, he reprised the role of "Mr. Ho" a wise sort of mystic who advises a man (played by Michael Keaton) facing the ramifications of a cancer diagnosis. Considering what he had survived and gone through in his earlier life, it truly was inspiring to see this man make something of himself in this manner.

On That Day

This life well lived would come to an end, when on February 25th, of 1996, Dr. Ngor was gunned down, right outside his residence, in Los Angeles, California. The killing was apparently a gang hit, and the gangsters were attempting to rob Ngor, when he refused to hand over a gold locket that contained a photo of his dead wife My-Huoy.

Ngor had been pushed around in his previous life by the Khmer Rouge thugs who wouldn't even allow him to treat his wife. If he had stood up to them it would have meant certain death, yet his wife and child still died in the process. Now that he was being bullied again by a bunch of two-bit hoodlums, he simply decided he wasn't going to be pushed around again. Even in the face of death, he refused to budge. While blood still ran in his veins, he refused to give up the memory of his dear wife. Sadly enough, it was after tussling over the locket that contained a photo of his former wife, My-Huoy, that Ngor was shot and killed.

The Suspects

The killers belonged to a local gang known as the "Oriental Lazy Boyz." Even though the case initially seemed like a clear-cut incident of gang violence. In later years, this synopsis of events would be called into question. For it was in 2009, that a former Khmer Rouge official—Kang Kek Iew—went on the record to claim that Dr. Ngo's death was an assassination ordered by none other than Pol Pot himself.

Pol Pot was apparently not happy with Dr. Ngo's activism and denunciation of the Khmer Rouge. According to Kang Kek, Pol Pot had used some of his contacts in the States, to orchestrate the hit, which was ultimately carried out by these gang bangers. Some of the oddities of Dr. Ngo's death seem to corroborate this account. For one thing, Ngo was found with some $2900 dollars in cold hard cash on his person.

If the gangsters' motives were robbery—why would they leave the cash? Were these killers not robbers, but rather hitmen? One could only imagine Dr. Ngo's shock. Imagine one of them approaching with a gun and shouting, "Hey! We've been sent to take you out! Under the orders of Pol Pot!" If such a hypothetical exchange ever did occur, Dr. Ngo must have wondered, how in the world he had ended up in such a situation. He had fled Cambodia to leave his old life behind—would it catch up to him like this?

In the End

Was the reach of the Khmer Rouge really that long? In another bizarre irony, the actual killers would be delivered a guilty verdict for the killing on April 16th, 1998, which just so happened to be right around the time that Pol Pot passed away. This Hollywood Homicide is as sad as it is mysterious—whole new chapters are still being written on Dr. Ngo; his life, as well as his death.

The Strange and Murderous End of Johnny Lewis

Who*:* Johnny Lewis
Where: Hollywood, California
When: September 2012
Suspects*:* Johnny Lewis
Conviction*:* Deceased

Background Information

Jonathan Kendrick Lewis—otherwise known as "Johnny" Lewis—was born on October 29th, 1983. Johnny hailed from North Hollywood, and even before he was famous had made Tinsel Town his own familiar stomping ground. Moving out of his parent's house at the age of 18, Johnny was still in his teens when he first started getting several walk-on roles on various TV shows such as "7th Heaven," "Malcolm in the Middle," "Boston Public," "The Guardian," "Yes, Dear," and "American Dreams."

He then made his way to the big screen, when he starred in the film "Raise Your Voice." He starred in this film opposite Hilary Duff. The film is set in Flagstaff, Arizona, and Hilary Duff plays the part of "Terri Fletcher." Terri Fletcher was a young girl with big dreams of becoming a star, even though her businessman father heartily disapproves.

Terri has to go behind her dad's back to continue to pursue her interests and those interests eventually introduce her to a DJ known as "Kiwi" It was Johnny Lewis who played the Kiwi character. Although this film was the primary vehicle to catapult Johnny Lewis to prominence, it was generally panned by critics who found it to be boring, bland, and utterly "formulaic" as it pertained to the structure of the plot.

Nevertheless, the following year Johnny was booked for the 2005 action/comedy film—"Underclassman." Although the movie contained the early star power of Nick Cannon, it too was a rather forgettable flop at the box office which earned a little over five million, even though its budget racked up over 25 million in expenses. It was after these two dismal films, that Johnny returned to his much more successful stomping ground of television.

He ended up scoring a recurring role in the TV show "Quintuplets" and also appeared on the Nickelodeon show "Drake & Josh." It was around this time, that he began a relationship with the already quite famous singing icon—Katy Perry. The two broke it off in 2006, but even that brief period with Perry—who herself was just on the verge of breaking out to the big time—seemed to raise Johnny's profile considerably.

104

In 2007, Johnny was quite busy working on films such as "Palo Alto" and even the latest installment of "Aliens vs. Predator." He also made an appearance on the hit show "Smallville." Life seemed good for Johnny and full of promise.

It was around this time, he entered into a relationship with an actress by the name of Diane Gaeta. The relationship was tumultuous however, and even though Diane ended up giving birth to Johnny's one and only child—they would ultimately go their separate ways and Johnny would see very little of the baby.

Even so, he would try to rebound and his acting career seemed to pick up when he was recruited to take part in "Sons of Anarchy," a drama series that ran for several seasons. Things were going well enough, but it was while he was working on the set of "Sons of Anarchy" that he suffered a bad motorcycle crash, that left him with a TBI (Traumatic Brain Injury).

Many who knew Johnny would later testify that he was never quite the same after this crash. And his behavior immediately afterward seems to suggest as much. For it was in the aftermath of this crash that he began to have frequent run-ins with the law. In January 2012 he ended up getting arrested for hitting a couple of guys with a bottle. He was then arrested just a few weeks later, for supposedly trying to bust into a lady's residence.

Even though he was way out of bounds in both of these crimes, he seemed to be cognizant enough to know that he didn't stand a chance; and as such, he pled "no contest." According to his dad, his son was acting increasingly odd and the whole family was deeply concerned about his behavior and was in the process of seeking an intervention. Johnny Lewis in the meantime, had moved into the Writers' Villa which had long provided lodging for local artists.

On That Day

The Writer's Villa was owned by Catherine Davis—a well-known figure in Hollywood, California. Catherine was 81 years old and had hob-knobbed with quite a few Hollywood celebrities in her day. But all of that would come to an end on September 26th, 2012, when, for reasons that remain unknown, Johnny viciously assaulted Davis and she was later found deceased from blunt force trauma.

Not only did Johnny kill her, but he also apparently killed her cat, which was discovered brutalized in another room. Just prior to killing his landlady, Ms. Davis, Johnny had already gotten into an altercation with his neighbors. He had apparently been snooping around next door when he got into an argument with another resident and a local handyman who just happened to be working on the property.

It was after this dustup, that he went straight to his landlady, Catherine's door, stormed in, and proceeded to beat her and her cat to death. Johnny Lewis had already been in quite a bit of trouble, but now he most likely would have faced severe repercussions—if he had lived long enough to face them. For shortly after his latest spate of mayhem, Johnny himself would die.

It remains unclear exactly what happened, but Johnny at some point had been out on Davis's patio and tumbled off of it. It's still not entirely clear if he did so on purpose or by accident; but regardless, the result was the same. As soon as he smacked into the pavement below, he was a goner. His death was ultimately ruled accidental—but like many of the mysterious Hollywood deaths mentioned in this book, there is still much that remains unknown.

In the End

It truly is bizarre to consider the last few moments of this promising Hollywood actor's life. He went on a brief but brutal rampage, bouncing around his neighborhood like a truly unhinged and homicidal maniac; only to fall, jump, or get pushed, off a ledge. The bizarre antics of Johnny's last day on Earth are surely stranger than any fictional script that any Hollywood writer could have ever cooked up.

The Bizarre Death
of Bob Saget

Who*:* Bob Saget
Where: Orlando, Florida
When: January 2022
Suspects*:* Unknown
Conviction*:* None

Background Information

If you grew up in the early 1990s, the name Bob Saget should be quite familiar to you. Because who could forget the TV Dad role he played as Danny Tanner, on the hit sitcom "Full House." Bob Saget played the part of a squeaky-clean widower father, doing the best he could to raise his three kids. This image is actually a pretty far cry from Bob Saget's actual personal life and career. Saget, prior to taking on this role earned his bread and butter as a stand-up comic. And a rather raunchy one at that.

Far from family-friendly—his jokes were almost always retrieved from somewhere in the gutter. Saget was born on May 17th, 1956, and far from the lights of Hollywood—he made his worldly debut in Philadelphia, Pennsylvania. Here he grew up the son of Benjamin and Rosalyn Saget. Both of his parents were successful, highly respected members of the community.

His father was the head of a chain of supermarkets, and his mother worked as an administrator at a local hospital. Most probably figured that Bob would follow in his parent's footsteps. But after graduating from high school, Bob Saget would become a film major at Temple University. He was studying how to produce movies, but in reality, Saget wanted to star in them.

In the meantime, while in college he was a regular at comedy clubs, where he developed a convincing sense of comedic timing. Saget ended up graduating from Temple University in 1978 and pursued a Hollywood career. His efforts would ultimately lead to him being given the role of Danny Tanner for "Full House" in 1987. Saget would remain with the long-running series until it was canceled in 1995.

Saget also worked as the host of a program in which viewers would submit funny home movies, which was aptly named, "America's Funniest Home Videos." He served as host of this program from 1989 to 1997. After leaving these two roles behind, Saget began to work behind the scenes, as a director. A new recurring TV role would then emerge for him in 2001, on the sitcom "Raising Dad." This TV series once again put Saget in the role of a widowed father raising two daughters.

If Saget felt typecast at this point, it seems he didn't mind. The TV show, however, proved to be nowhere near as successful as "Full House" had been, and ended in 2002, less than a year after its premiere. Bob Saget had more success with the comedy show "How I Met Your Mother."

For this sitcom, he actually did some voice acting as an unseen narrator of events. Although he wouldn't be seen for the part he played—it would give him a lasting gig until the program was canceled in 2014. Bob Saget was then free to pursue his old passion—stand-up comedy—over the next couple of years. Surprising just about everyone, Saget would then be tapped in 2016 to reprise his role as Danny Tanner, for the updated version of "Full House," which had been rebranded as "Fuller House."

Saget would ride out this wave until 2020. Saget in the meantime, had remarried. His first marriage was to Sherri Kramer (married from 1982 to 1997) with whom he had three children. His second marriage, however, was to Kelly Rizzo, whom he married in 2018. Saget would remain married to Kelly until his untimely demise in 2022.

On That Day

It was on January 9th, 2022, that Bob Saget died. Saget was on tour, doing stand-up comedy, when his body was discovered in his hotel room in the Ritz Carlton of Orlando, Florida. His cause of death remains mysterious with very few details. An official autopsy, however, has confirmed that his cause of death was "blunt head trauma." Saget somehow received a tremendous blow to the back of his head and had fractures around his eyes.

It's since been said Bob had some sort of freak accident, although how the determination of this has been made remains unclear. Not helping suspicions, is the fact that one of the doctors that examined Saget went on the record to state that it looked like he was hit on the side of the head with a baseball bat, causing severe fracturing. And this was no random physician saying this, but rather the Chief Medical Examiner—Dr. Joshua Stephany.

The Investigation

It is indeed somewhat perplexing (some might say suspicious) to be told that this man died of an accident, and then have an examining doctor seem to suggest that he was whacked with a Louisville slugger! So, which is it? Did Saget fall down and hit his head, only to crawl into bed and die? Or did something much more sinister happen? Investigators who typically jump at the chance to look into the murder angle, have been strangely quiet on this one.

Seeming to take no for an answer—they even caved when Bob Saget's wife demanded they refrain from releasing information about the autopsy. Saget's wife cited privacy concerns, but many others couldn't help but wonder if she had something else in mind. Any denial of details in a case like this of course inevitably leads to suspicions of a cover-up. Even stranger is how quickly authorities were to go out of their way to declare that there was "no sign of foul play."

But oddly enough, there aren't any real signs of an accident for that matter either. According to investigators, if Saget fell and hit his head, it most likely occurred inside his hotel room. Yet, just a cursory examination of the digs in Saget's room reveal that it had plush carpeting, very soft to the touch. Even the headboard of the bed he slept in was padded. There simply wasn't much at all in the way of hard surfaces for Saget to hit his head on. So, just how did his injury occur?

Typically, in a case with so many unusual features as this one—investigators are eager to follow any potentially suspicious leads, wherever they may take them. Yet despite the fact that Saget died of blunt force trauma as if he were hit on the head with a baseball bat, all those involved seemed all too eager to wash their hands of Saget's death.

Wash their hand of his death and essentially declare, "Nothing to see here folks! Everything's just fine! No foul play at all!" It's enough to make us ask the question: Was Bob Saget's death a tragic accident, or yet another Hollywood Homicide, conveniently swept under the rug?

Lloyd Avery II
Boyz n the Hood to
Hollywood Homicide

Who*:* Lloyd Avery II
Where: Los Angeles, California
When: September 2005
Suspects*:* Kevin Roby
Conviction*:* None (Already serving life for previous offense)

Background Information

He's best known for a short appearance he made on the epic 1991 Hollywood production of "Boyz n the Hood." Lloyd Avery II played the part of a character whose part was initially considered so small that he didn't even get a name. The script simply listed him as "Knucklehead." In other words, as just some random, belligerent, tough guy gangster. Avery played the part so convincingly, however, that this small role would take on a larger-than-life memory for the movie-going audience.

Many could hardly forget the stunning scene in which Avery's character hops out of a car wielding a sawn-off shotgun, with full intensity in his eyes, right before he delivers the death blow to the main character, "Ricky." Yes, Avery would forever go down as *the guy who shot Ricky.* But all of this, of course, was just acting. Avery wasn't a gangster in real life, right? Well, he wasn't originally.

He was born in a fairly well-off family in fact, in an up-and-coming neighborhood of Los Angeles. His dad was a veteran plumber, carpenter, and electrician, who had started his own successful business. He made so much money, that his mom didn't have to work, and stayed home to make sure that the children were well cared for. The Averys had all of their needs taken care of and even a swimming pool in the backyard. This was not a family that did without, and Avery had every opportunity to succeed in life.

111

Lloyd Avery II attended Beverly Hills High School, where by all accounts he was a popular, well-adjusted kid, who did well in both sports and academic study. He had achieved some greatness in fact in baseball and water polo—receiving his lettered jacket for both. He was remembered as a fun guy to be around with a great sense of humor, often seen cutting up during class. The worst trouble he ever got into was at the high school parties he was invited to.

These parties were typically held when some rich classmate's parents were out of town, and the home-alone teenager decided to throw a spontaneous bash now that they had the mansion to themselves. These rich kids would drink and perhaps do some drugs. Avery wasn't the instigator of any of this, of course, he was just tagging along for the ride. Despite his penchant for attending parties, however, there was absolutely no sign of the trouble to come.

And furthermore, Avery, with his squeaky clean, rich kid background, had no connection whatsoever with gang life. It wasn't until he was tapped to cameo on "Boyz n the Hood" in 1991, that Avery seemed to somehow develop an interest. One can only speculate, but perhaps Avery felt somehow isolated and cut off from the real action from his affluent perch, and something about the gang world he was introduced to while filming "Boyz n the Hood" really appealed to him.

It was shortly after filming wrapped up that Avery seemed to have become a changed man. He was recruited for the role seemingly at random. Avery had met and befriended the screenwriter and director John Singleton, a film school grad. from USC. Singleton had just secured approval to begin production of "Boyz n the Hood," and he needed to beef up his list of cast members. Avery, on what was almost a lark, agreed to take on a small part in the film.

From the beginning of shooting, John Singleton sought to guide Lloyd Avery into the role, showing him just how to hold his weapon, how to look into the camera, and otherwise convey emotion. Avery seemed to be a natural and picked up on all of the subtle cues used by great actors, quite easily. But not everyone was so receptive to Avery. It would later be recalled that Cuba Gooding Jr., who was a rising star at the time, had a dustup with Avery for what seemed to be no particular reason.

Avery had simply said "hi" to him in fact, only for an agitated Cuba Gooding to snap at him, "Don't f**** talk to me right now!"

Sadly, many celebrities develop too much ego for their own good. And Gooding seemed to think that since he was already a big star, he didn't have the time to chat with the extras hired for small bit parts. Avery wasn't about to take any stuff from Gooding however, and the two seemed on the verge of actually coming to blows. It was only with the help of other cast members and crew, that the scuffle was broken up.

Nevertheless, the film was indeed finished, and "Boyz n the Hood" was a great success at the box office. Not only that, it made Avery a local legend in Los Angeles. He was recognized on the street, and given all the perks that come with celebrity. He would get into the best nightclubs for free and be greeted with praise from fans who loved his performance.

His future seemed bright, and he already had another movie role lined up, in which he once again played a gun-toting gang-banger, for Singleton's next release "Poetic Justice." This film was far less memorable than "Boyz n the Hood" however, and would ultimately bomb at the box office.

Lloyd Avery II himself thought the film was lousy, and during its premiere which he attended along with John Singleton and the other cast members, he actually stood up and booed his own movie. It's said that as soon as the film ended, he expressed his disgust by standing up out of his seat and shouting at John Singleton, "This shit was whack, John!"

It was after this failed film that Lloyd Avery II fully delved into street life, and began to live out the fantasy he long harbored about being a real-life gangster. Even so, he still had connections to Hollywood, and still occasionally talked with Singleton about future projects. And eventually, he would be tapped to take part in the 1999 movie—"Lockdown."

Here he would play the part of a man coming to grips with the hard reality of prison life. It wasn't a very uplifting role, but Avery appreciated the gritty realness of it. Avery proved to be quite disastrous on the set of this movie, however. He had a short temper and often got into altercations with other cast members. Things got so bad in fact, that many of Avery's scenes were cut out, and his role in the movie was considerably downsized.

Because of his own antics, what could have been a breakthrough role was relegated once again to just a few meager bit parts. The most ridiculous part of Lloyd Avery's stint in "Lockdown" actually occurred the day he has fired from the set altogether. Filming was wrapping up when Lloyd Avery II decided to steal a boom box from a cast member and sit on the back of a truck blasting music with it. He was not only taking in tunes from a stolen radio but also smoking pot laced with embalming fluid.

It was after he was asked to give the radio back, that Avery suddenly tried to attack a member of the crew. He was stopped by several others, however, and chased off the set. Bizarrely enough, the stoned and belligerent Avery then ran right up to a local prison. Lloyd Avery II was still in character for "Lockdown," and dressed like a prison inmate, in a jumpsuit. It was while dressed up in his prison garb that he scaled a tower and attempted to *break into* a real-life prison.

The guards who were trained to keep folks from breaking out likely had no idea what to make of someone trying to break into their facility. With their guns drawn and aimed at Avery, they weren't messing around. It was only when some of the set members strolled up and carefully explained the situation, that cooler heads were able to prevail. Avery was ordered to get down and advised to leave the area at once. Many might have assumed that this bizarre episode would have all but spelled the end of Avery's acting career.

But it wasn't the end… Avery still had another film lined up. He was recruited to play another gangster for the film "Shot." For this film, he played the part of a character called "G-Ride." For this film, Avery had cleaned up his act considerably and seemed to take his acting much more seriously. He worked hard and hoped that this film would be a great representation of what life on the streets of LA was really like.

But again, the portrayal that Avery was making as "G-Ride" was greatly blurring Avery's perception of the separation between art and life. Avery was still gang-banging on the side, and it was during the production of this film that he actually killed two people during a drug deal gone bad. No one on set knew that they were working with a murderer, but Avery knew the dark secrets of what he had done, and yet carried on with his acting as if it didn't matter.

It did though. And on December 8th, 1999 he was arrested on suspicions of committing a double homicide. Avery then went on trial in 2000 and was found guilty as charged. He was given a life sentence for his crimes and began serving his term at Pelican Bay prison in 2001. This wasn't the end of the story, however, for Avery himself would ultimately become a Hollywood homicide.

On That Day

For it was on September 4th, 2005, when Avery was 36 years of age, that his cellmate, a self-proclaimed Satanist by the name of Kevin Roby, choked Avery to death in their cell. Prior to his death, Avery had become active with Christian groups at the prison. Avery in fact, seemed to have had a late-life conversion and had placed his focus fully on God and redemption. Avery was so enthused about Christianity in fact, that inmates had nicknamed him "Baby Jesus."

The Suspect

It is indeed strangely ironic that prison officials would place a guy called "Baby Jesus" in a cell with a self-proclaimed Satanist. Kevin Roby and Lloyd Avery II inevitably had a conflict. And even though Avery tried his best to preach the Good News of the Gospel to Roby—this Satanist just wasn't having it.

And after killing Avery, the crazed Roby insisted that he killed Avery as a further "warning to God." As if, killing a man deeply steeped and enriched in the Christian faith would somehow send a message to the Almighty himself. Such things are clearly the ramblings of a demented, twisted, and murderous mind. But whatever the case may be, the death of Lloyd Avery II, already convicted of two Hollywood homicides, makes three.

Right Around the Corner

The life of celebrities is by its very nature a fleeting enterprise. They are on top, feature on all the magazine covers, and are the talk of the town. The next thing they know, they are old news. Or even worse, they become tabloid fodder. No longer notable for their stunning exploits, they are only remembered for the drama of their own out-of-control personal lives.

There have been many celebrities that have risen and fallen in this manner. Elvis Presley and Michael Jackson are among the most notable. These stars had it all - fortune, fame, and high praise - only to be openly ridiculed at the end of their days. And as bad as some of their lives end up - the deaths of some celebrities are not much better.

Kurt Cobain, John Lennon, and Kid McCoy all faced an abrupt and sad end. Two of them supposedly by their own hand - at least according to the official rendering of events - and one was shot multiple times in the back by a deranged fan.

It can be a rough and tumble world for a celebrity, but most no doubt never bargained for the tumultuous lives and untimely deaths they faced. Yes, they are rich and famous, but they are not bulletproof. And as the many stories in this book have demonstrated, the famous can be just as vulnerable as anyone else.

Perhaps that's why the deaths of superstars are so shocking. In a strange way, it reminds us of our own mortality. For if these larger-than-life figures can be knocked down so easily - where does that leave the rest of us? If they are here today and gone tomorrow, then no doubt the same could be said for any one of us. It's sad but true - and the Hollywood headlines only serve as a reminder that the grim reaper could be right around the corner.

Further Readings

Now that this book has reached its conclusion, feel free to take a look at some of the reading and reference materials that helped make it all possible. Here you will find a wide variety of facts and opinions about the cases presented here in this book.

The Hollywood Scandal Almanac. Roberts, Jerry
This text provides a great overview of many of the scandals that have rocked Hollywood throughout the years. It's a great resource for many of the cases covered in this book.

Thomas Ince: Hollywood's Independent Pioneer. Taves, Brian
This particular book follows the life of Thomas Ince. Here you will find a comprehensive telling of his entire life story.

Buzz: The Life and Art of Busby Berkeley. Spivak, Jeffrey
Yet another biography—this time pertaining to the often troubled life of Busby Berkeley.

Murders of Hollywood: A Collection of True Crime. Fona, Laura
This is a fairly useful anthology of Hollywood True Crime.

Celebrity Murders and Other Nefarious Deeds. Max, Haines
This book provides an interesting anthology of celebrity-involved murders and other crimes. It's worth taking a second look.

Love & Death: The Murder of Kurt Cobain. Wallace Max and Halperin, Ian
Here in this book, Ian Halperin; a seasoned music journalist takes a look at Kurt Cobain, his relationship with Courtney Love, and the subsequent talk and theories over his untimely death.

Bless You, Bollywood! A Tribute to Hindi Cinema on Completing 100 Years. Rishi, Tilak
This book relates the history of Bollywood and its actors— including the late Tilak Rishi.

I Don't Want to Live This Life: A Mother's Story of Her Daughter's Murder. Spungen, Deborah
This is a book about Nancy Spungen, detailing her life as recalled by her own mother; Deborah Spungen.

Jam Master Jay: The Heart of Hip Hop. Thigpen, David
Here in this book, David Thigpen recounts the life and untimely death of Run DMC's Jam Master Jay.

Image Credits

Lord Byron image
By Thomas Phillips - BBC Your Paintings, Public Domain,
https://commons.wikimedia.org/w/index.php?curid=11540297

Edgar Allan Poe
By Unknown author; Restored by Yann Forget and Adam Cuerden - Derived from
File:Edgar Allan Poe, circa 1849, restored.jpg; originally from
http://www.getty.edu/art/gettyguide/artObjectDetails?artobj=39406, Public Domain,
https://commons.wikimedia.org/w/index.php?curid=77527076

Kid McCoy image
By Los Angeles Times - https://digital.library.ucla.edu/catalog/ark:/21198/zz0002pjb1,
CC BY 4.0, https://commons.wikimedia.org/w/index.php?curid=122057899

Kurt Cobain image
By P.B. Rage from USA - More Kurt -- too rad, CC BY-SA 2.0,
https://commons.wikimedia.org/w/index.php?curid=121644185

Divya Bharti image
By మురళీకృష్ణ ఐ మునుసునూరి - Own work, CC BY-SA 4.0,

https://commons.wikimedia.org/w/index.php?curid=116163245

Bobbi Kristina Brown
By Asterio Tecson - This file has been extracted from another file, CC BY-SA 2.0,
https://commons.wikimedia.org/w/index.php?curid=59282849

Jack Nance image
By Libra Films - This file has been extracted from another file, Public Domain,
https://commons.wikimedia.org/w/index.php?curid=90082271

John Lennon image
By Eric Koch, Nationaal Archief, Den Haag, Rijksfotoarchief: Fotocollectie Algemeen
Nederlands Fotopersbureau (ANEFO), 1945-1989 - negatiefstroken zwart/wit, nummer
toegang 2.24.01.05, bestanddeelnummer 916-5098 - Nationaal Archief, CC BY-SA 3.0
nl, https://commons.wikimedia.org/w/index.php?curid=76225784

Sean Taylor image
By dbking of flickr - https://www.flickr.com/photos/bootbearwdc/32500141/, CC BY 2.0,
https://commons.wikimedia.org/w/index.php?curid=2346339

Thomas Ince image
By Fred Hartsook (1876–1930) - picturesofcelebrities.com, Public Domain,
https://commons.wikimedia.org/w/index.php?curid=84140837

Busby Berkeley image

Made in the USA
Coppell, TX
05 October 2024